T0147523

BOOM, BUST & BEYOND

BOOM, BUST & BEYOND
Winning Real Estate Strategy in the 2010s

Chester W. "Chet" Allen, CCIM, SEC, EMS

iUniverse, Inc.
New York   Bloomington

Boom, Bust & Beyond
Winning Real Estate Strategy in the 2010s

iUniverse books may be ordered through booksellers or by contacting:

iUniverse
1663 Liberty Drive
Bloomington, IN 47403
www.iuniverse.com
1-800-Authors (1-800-288-4677)

Because of the dynamic nature of the Internet, any Web addresses or links contained in this book may have changed since publication and may no longer be valid. The views expressed in this work are solely those of the author and do not necessarily reflect the views of the publisher, and the publisher hereby disclaims any responsibility for them.

ISBN: 978-1-4502-2001-9 (sc)
ISBN: 978-1-4502-2002-6 (ebk)

Printed in the United States of America

iUniverse rev. date: 06/08/2010

Foreword

My previous real estate book, The Guide to Becoming Real Estate Rich, was written in 1999 and the foreword contended that while there were fortunes being made in dot-com investments, real estate historically had a better track record than any other type of investment. Somewhere in the book, I contended that real estate, nationally, would never substantially decrease in value because most owners didn't have to sell and would not do so at a large loss.

Although I have been a real estate investment broker, developer, builder and investor for over 40 years, and a veteran of three other recessions, nothing in my experience compares with the turmoil of the 2007-2009 years.

The years between 1999 and this writing have been filled with unprecedented events. In 1999, California and much of the nation was recovering from a major real estate recession. Brokers and builders were barely hanging on—the 1993 Builder's Association's Convention motto was "stay alive 'til '95." By 1999, the real estate market was on the upswing, and the next seven years recorded unprecedented property appreciation, far beyond my previous experience.

And I was in the right place at the right time with the right team. A group of us formed a development corporation and hit home run after home run, recording huge profits for ourselves and our investors. Our properties were appreciating 1-5% per month, and buyers were flocking to acquire our homes and condos. Financing had never been easier and the "flippers" were making tens of thousands, sometimes without ever going into title.

Our team was made up of real estate veterans: we had all survived the ups and downs of previous "cycles." One of our mission statements was not to be highly leveraged and non-liquid when the appreciation (boom) inevitably stopped and properties quit selling.

What we, and most of the country's other developers, couldn't control was the lead time project processing was taking. When I first started developing real estate, I could get a subdivision approved in six weeks and a building permit in a few hours. With an onslaught of state regulations, required environmental impact reports, protesters, understaffed city building and planning departments and utility providers, projects in California and many other states were taking years to get approved. To tie up a potentially productive parcel of land in boom times requires quick action and large, non-refundable deposits. To attract investors, a construction lender needs to be in place. Entitling a major development project require hundreds of thousands, even millions, of up-front investment dollars and loan commitments.

The bottom line is that the developer can't just stop. There are some who saw the writing on the wall, didn't acquire any land, and sat on the sidelines during the end of the 2000-2006 boom. The rest of us got caught, and it cost us millions.

And the banks got caught too, even worse. Standard bank policy on construction lending was to make a 75% of value or 80% of cost loan, whichever was less. On a project slated to sell out at $12,000,000, with a cost of $10,000,000, the bank would lend $8,000,000 (80% of $10,000,000), not $9,000,000 (75% of $12,000,000).

When the market dried up and properties went down 40% in value, the developer and investors lost all of their investment, and the bank was stuck with an unsold (and probably unfinished) project that they had all, or much of their $8,000,000 already in. The developer and his investors were broke, and there were no other healthy developers ready to buy the project, except possibly at vulture prices. If the bank has enough of these bad loans, the bank goes under, too.

Now we are beginning a new decade. Inflation looms. Prices are back to reality. Real estate is ready to again take its place as the best of all investments.

Table of Contents

Chapter 1
Beyond

I have now been through four recessions as a real estate professional. They have all been unique, in both their cause and recovery. In the depths of each, we, who were players at the time, couldn't see the light at the end of the tunnel. We didn't know that there would be a recovery. We didn't know whether we were at the bottom, or whether it would get worse. Every boom was different, every bust was different, and each beyond took on a unique life of its own.

And the Great Recession of 2007-? is, if anything, more unpredictable. Daily newspapers and television reporters have conflicting articles. Things are getting better. Things are getting worse. I receive e-mails saying our financial system is doomed. Others tell me that opportunities have never been greater.

A new term has been created—"reset." I heard it first on television from Tom Brokaw. His observation was that this time we weren't just in a "cycle," but the country, and maybe the world was going to reset, and the economic fundamentals would make a paradigm change. The reset would affect our conspicuous consumption habits. We would no longer need 4,000 square foot homes, multiple automobiles and many of the toys we began to feel were necessities in the early 2000s. We would begin to save instead of taking on unmanageable credit. Family units would become closer.

Whatever the outcome of The Great Recession, several fundamentals regarding real estate as an investment have become clear.

Real estate can either be an investment, based on a solid foundation, or it can be pure speculation. The majority of this book is a how to guide for responsibly investing in real estate, and how to measure and mitigate risk.

Where real estate and business "investing" get into trouble is when profit expectations are based purely on appreciation, which can be greatly magnified by leverage. We will be covering the risk-rewards of leverage and appreciation later, but overpaying for a business (stocks) or real estate simply because everyone is doing it ultimately leads to bust.

At last count, prices of single family residences in San Diego County were about the same as they were in 2002. This is after a loss of 35% from their highest (2006) prices. What happened between 2002 and 2006 to cause an increase in prices of 35%, or roughly 8-10% annually? It was not that homebuyers could afford to pay 35% more for their homes (although cheaper credit did help), but that speculators believed home prices would go up and up, and kept buying, no matter what the price.

One of the last subdivisions we built before the bust was a fairly upscale development of homes in the Palm Springs area of California, primarily designed to be first homes for retired and white collar workers and second homes for "snowbirds," those who wanted the warm winters on California's desert recreation paradise. As it turned out, approximately 1/3rd of the 33 homes we built were sold to full time residents, 1/3rd as second homes, and 1/3rd to speculators. Many of the speculators had a game plan. Buy into the first phase of any development, because the prices of the subsequent phases would be higher. If they could buy a $700,000 home for little or nothing down, and the next phase came out at $770,000, they could flip their investment and make a quick $70,000 profit, or wait for the third phase and make a $140,000 profit.

Ultimately, a sustainable market rests on affordability. Who can afford to use an inflated valued property? The real value of a commodity comes back to what a user can afford to pay to own or use a product.

Starting with homes, what can an average working family afford to pay in rent or mortgage payment to occupy a property? Obviously the specific dollar amount is all over the board depending on each family's income, but as there are only so many users in each income bracket, increasing product prices will eventually dry up the number of users.

In commercial properties, tenants have a limit on what they can afford to pay in rent without going broke. Top leasing agents may be great at stealing tenants for a new shopping center or office building, but the vacancies left behind will ultimately impact commercial values.

So, back to reset. Once the banks and financial institutions straighten out their lending strategies, real estate prices will have to return to user affordability. And this won't be easy. There are several major obstacles.

First there are the governmental agencies, and utilities. City and county governments depend on processing fees to help balance their budgets. Building permit fees for just one home can range from $2,000 to $200,000. The cost to subdivide, entitle, and develop a tract can exceed $135,000 per lot.

And then there is resistance to change. The term NIMBY is an acronym for Not In My BackYard. Neighborhood resistance and communities' fear of lawsuits drive the cost of entitling projects out of sight, and the delays have doomed scores of developers and builders.

Real estate itself has changed dramatically since I built my first building in Alaska in 1958. Alaska had just become a state, and if you wanted to build something, you just did it. There were no planning staffs, no zoning, no inspectors, and no permits. You bought a parcel of land, and built on it. Or you subdivided it. You had the right to do whatever you wanted with your land.

Most of the "lower 48" were already more restrictive at that time, and did have zoning, building permitting and building inspectors. But, absent health and safety issues, property owners were pretty well allowed to do what they wanted with their properties.

In most states today, there is no such thing as unrestricted real estate ownership. No matter what the owner paid for the property or how long they have owned it, the only right the owner has is to do what the community tells the owner can be done with it. If you want to build a house, the community must approve all the plans and even the look of the structure. Or they can disapprove, and the owner is faced with paying property taxes for an unusable property.

We were recently in negotiations with Walmart to sell a partnership property for a new store. Because they are always sued by somebody, Walmart requires a four year escrow. They have learned from experience that they can't just go through normal processing: they have to do a full blown Environmental Impact Report and will have to defend at least one lawsuit before being able to start building.

Returning to an era of user affordability will not be easy. Land owners will need to rethink their land values, and be more receptive to developer's time problems.

Rehabbing existing properties can be a major play in reinstituting user affordability. One of our companies International Vacancy Exchange (www.vacancyexchange.com) motto is that "Half the World is Vacancies." It may be more or less than half, but the reality is that there are millions of existing square feet of retail, office, industrial, self storage, hotel rooms and land that are not being used.

Maybe we builders, developers, agents and investors will revert to old cyclical habits, but hopefully the bust of the Great Recession will make us re-examine user affordability, and the real value of real estate.

Most of the fundamental truths about real estate still apply.

For hundreds of years real estate has been the primary vehicle for estate building. If not still primary, real estate investing and developing is certainly the number one alternative to the highly volatile stock market.

Chapter 2
Timing

Discussing his success, a large shopping center developer put it very simply, "It's all in the timing." The most thorough investor, the most intelligent developer, even cautious homeowners get burned if their timing is wrong. And totally unsophisticated bumblers make it big, when their timing is right.

Real estate wealth is the child of economic cycles. And the wonderful thing about real estate investing is that money, big money, can be made in both boom and bust times. The key is positioning oneself to take advantage of the current stage of the economic cycle.

Buyers' Markets and Sellers' Markets

Buyers' Market

A buyers' market occurs when there are more properties on the market than buyers for those properties, typically after periods of overbuilding and during recessions. During these times, property values are stable or decreasing. Owners get desperate. In severely depressed markets, foreclosures occur. Lenders dump properties, and a downward spiral of pricing occurs. Properties might remain on the market for months and even years.

During the Great Depression of the 1930s the entire country was mired in this stagnant type of market. Since World War II, until the Great Recession of 2007-?, recessionary markets have tended only to impact certain regions or employees of certain industries. The entire country was affected at various points, but not simultaneously. That changed in 2009: all sections of the country were affected, some much more than others. Southern California, Las Vegas, Nevada, Phoenix, Arizona and Florida, areas that received the most speculative growth, crashed far worse than more conservative areas such as Indiana and upstate New York.

In the late 1970s mid-western farm prices plummeted. About the same time, the northeast "rustbelt" states were dying because of foreign competition. While the mid-west and northeast were depressed, jobs and opportunities were plentiful in the go-go southwest. Then, in the 1980s, energy prices fell— Texas, Colorado and the rest of what had formerly been the national bright spot, took a terrible economic beating. In 1990 it was California's turn. California, which had hardly felt the woes of the rest of the nation during the 70s and 80s, fell to the multiple curses of high prices, defense cutbacks, and a worldwide recession.

Certain types of real estate can suffer nationally. Office buildings, overbuilt in the tax-shelter heydays of the early 1980s, lost their allure for a decade following the passage of the tax reform act in 1986. Most metropolitan areas experienced greater than 20% office vacancies and the term "see-through" buildings was born to describe their empty appearance. At the same time, in many of the same communities, well-located apartment buildings maintained, and even increased, their value and investment desirability.

Sellers' Market
A Sellers' Market occurs when there are more buyers than properties on the market for sale. During these times, prices accelerate rapidly and many properties remain on the market for only a few days.

California, in the mid 1980s, late 1990s and early 2000s, was embroiled in a sellers' market. Money was plentiful, properties scarce, and the future bright. Homes increased in value 1% or more per month and buyers were waiting in line. Home prices became grossly inflated. One survey showed that only 2% of the homeowners in the San Francisco Bay area could afford, or qualify, to buy the home they were occupying if they had to do so at the then current market prices.

Apartment buildings were popular amongst buyers and many were selling at such high prices (and low yields) that they made no economic sense. The same was true of other income property. Shopping centers were going up on nearly every corner and investors and lenders were throwing money at the product, all betting on the future.

Pressure on developers to acquire ready-to-go, zoned land drove land prices skyward, and those prices, combined with higher development fees (the cities were getting their fingers in the pot, too) drove prices of homes, apartments and other investment properties even higher.

This is not to say that money can't be made buying in a sellers' market. Like the stock market, fortunes can be made by shrewd investors, jumping in during an up-market and riding it for a period of time. However, to successfully play this real estate speculation game, the investor had better know when to jump off.

During these crazy inflationary times we coined what we called "the greater fool theory": it was okay to buy an overpriced property because it could be resold in a few months (and sometimes, even in the same escrow) for a substantial profit to an even "greater fool."

I knew of one development land parcel that had four different sales going at one time. "A" sold to "B" for $8,000 per acre, escrow to close in 60 days. Ten days later "B" contracted with "C" to sell the property at $10,000 per acre, 50 day close. Five days later "C" contracted with

"D" to sell the property at $12,000 per acre, 45 day close. And finally "D" made a deal with "E" at $15,000 per acre.

When the bottom fell out of the California market it was like the children's game of musical chairs. The last "greater fool" didn't have a seat.

Four years and tens of thousands of dollars spent earning an Economics degree at Stanford and the only thing I remember is the adage most of us learned by the second grade; "Buy low, sell high." It should come as no surprise that this is the key to becoming wealthy through real estate.

It is next to impossible to buy low in a Sellers' Market. In a true sellers' market it is not uncommon for sellers to receive multiple offers-to-purchase within hours of a property being listed. So why would any seller be willing to made a special, killer deal for you when they know there is another, eager buyer waiting in the wings with cash in hand.

But in a Buyers' Market, deals abound. Home-sites in Northern San Diego County that would have sold in a heartbeat for $125,000 in the up-swing year of 1989 were offered in the down-swing year of 1994 for $50,000 with no takers. Lenders were placing their foreclosed homes and income properties on the market at prices far less than the loans they had placed on these same properties just four years previously and were negotiating sales prices substantially lower than the listed bargain prices.

Buy low. But that is only half of the formula. The other half is sell high. And a Buyers' Market is not the time to sell high.

During recessions, when my real estate brokerage company advertised repossessed homes for sale, we continually received ad calls from potential investors who wanted to acquire "fixers" that, with a little cosmetic repair, could be re-marketed in a few months for a $25,000 profit. We didn't even attempt to work with those buyers. Oh, yes, we did counsel them.

We explained to those callers that there are outstanding long-term profits to be made acquiring selective fixers at bargain prices, provided they are willing to hold the properties until the market rebounds. Attempting to immediately resell their newly rehabbed property for any profit during a Buyers' Market would prove to be an exercise in futility.

Huge profits are made by those who buy in the depths of the Buyers' Market and then sell near the peaks of the following Sellers' Market.

Playing the Cycles

Before 2000, my experience showed that, nationally, real estate runs in roughly ten-year cycles. Articles written by statisticians document that the average economic cycle is less than that, but during my 45 year developing, building and brokering career, I recall recessions around 1970, 1980 and 1990, with the "good times" falling in the middle of those decades. The first decade of the 2000s has proved to be an exception, with the duration of the good times at least double that of the bad times.

What is a good time for real estate? Most people owning real estate would submit that it is when real estate appreciates in value—a Seller's Market. Times are good because owners can sell at a profit.

Available, affordable financing is a key element in a Sellers' Market. 1980 brought inflation—usually good for those owning real property—but the inflation was accompanied by historically high interest rates, which killed the real estate market.

As discussed earlier, it is important to remember that not all types of real estate and not all regions experience good times at the same time. It is quite probable that one area of the country will be experiencing good times while another is in the depths of a recession. And, within the same city, office buildings may be impossible to sell and finance, while the new home market is flourishing.

The lesson, then, is one of common sense. Buy when sellers are desperate. Sell when buyers are plentiful, loaded, and eager. Making a fortune in real estate is really quite easy because of the cycles. It would be much more difficult if we only had the good times.

Although playing the cycles is the prime ingredient for acquiring and keeping wealth, it is not the whole recipe. There are traps. Ghost towns exist. Industries die. The successful player is not just a one trick pony, only playing the markets. The winning player still needs to approach all aspects of the investment: examining locations, industries and money markets, as well as state of the economy.

In the following chapters we will be covering all facets of real estate as an investment, including a chapter discussing the available kinds of real estate and the potential opportunities and problems inherent with each.

Chapter 3
Investment Fundamentals

Once upon a time a very successful developer hired me to assist in marketing his one unsuccessful project. Handsomely designed, located on a prime site in one of the world's most beautiful locations, built and furnished by skilled craftsmen using the finest materials, the project hadn't sold and it was presently costing the developer in excess of $3,000,000 annually.

I, too, had been a principal in a very unsuccessful development project that had created a severe "net worth ectomy." A lodge in the Rocky Mountains had cost me most of my cash, two years of productivity and a very valuable parcel of California land that I had pledged.

One day, while having lunch with my developer client and his wife, I was asked, "As smart as you are, Chet, how did you possibly invest in that lodge project?"

"I got so caught up in the creativity of making the transaction that I forgot about the economics," was my reply.

Whereupon the wife turned to her husband and, with a rueful smile, said, "It sounds like somebody else I know."

If we are to amass and retain wealth through real estate investing, we must understand real estate investment fundamentals, and then discipline ourselves to insure that all of the properties and projects we seriously consider are sound economically. Players in the real estate game are exposed to hundreds of properties, many of which are pretty, some in superb locations, and most of which make no financial sense. To be successful, we must look beyond physical appearances and refrain from emotional decisions.

OVERVIEW

The real estate game, properly played, can be the most fun—and profitable—game in town. There are more moves than chess, more unknowns than poker, and the odds weigh heavily in favor of the intelligent player. Unlike most money games, the real estate investor has a great deal of control over his or her investment. Players in the stock and bond markets are dependent on the management skills of unknown third parties whose motives and loyalties are often suspect. The real estate investor can choose when and where to acquire, when and if to upgrade, when and if to raise rents or subdivide or condo. He or she can change management. But most importantly, the real estate investor has only his or her own best interests at heart.

Historically, real estate has been the most profitable of investments. The reasons are simple. First, there is a limited supply and ever increasing demand. Second, inflation drives up the costs of new construction and replacement of existing structures. And, finally, the attitude of real estate owners is one of positive expectancy.

Except during brief periods of severe recession, few who own real estate expect to sell for less than the purchase price. We all expect to make a profit. Therefore, most of us won't sell at a loss. If the market gets soft, the majority of real estate owners wait until it firms up. After all, historically it has always firmed up. We know we live in a cyclical economic world. Yes, real estate prices do go down temporarily. This occurs when a critical number of property owners lose confidence or must sell at the same time. This will happen if and when there is extensive overbuilding with resultant vacancies, and in times of economic downturns.

This is not to say that real estate investments don't have shortcomings; they do. The two most glaring shortcomings are the lack of instant liquidity and management. But even these can be mitigated or in some cases eliminated by choosing certain types of investments.

Real estate ownership advantages far outweigh its disadvantages. Besides the appreciation most long-time investors have come to expect, many real estate investments offer outstanding yields and others offer tax sheltered income. Equally important, real estate offers a unique vehicle for building and preserving one's estate—the tax deferred exchange, which will be covered later.

RISK VS RETURN

Good financial planning requires goal setting. For the real estate investor this involves determining a financial target and creating a timetable. Aggressive goals and short timetables dictate the need for high yields, or annual returns. It is an axiom (or should be) of all investments that "the higher the return, the higher the risk." It is not realistic to expect a secure investment such as a leased telephone building to offer the same high yield as an over-financed locally-owned fast food franchise. Post offices may not pencil out to be as potentially profitable as hillside condominium developments, but they are a whole lot safer!

GROWTH VS YIELD

Real estate players invest for different reasons, but the yardstick for success for most players is "How much money did you make?" Or, more importantly, "How much did you make and keep or preserve?" Real estate investments are usually purchased for their yield (annual return), and often correctly so, but the real profit in real estate investments is in the appreciation of the real estate (growth). As in the stock market, often the best yield investment is not the best growth investment.

Let me illustrate the distinction. Examine what occurred with California Bay Area home and apartment ownership during the middle 1970s, the 1980s and the post-recession 1990s and the early 2000s. Not only did highly leveraged houses produce no cash flow, but the investor had to make monthly cash infusions just to cover the loan payments. This is called "feeding," and the investment is known as an "eater." If the investment is a big enough eater, one that consumes prodigious quantities of cash each month, it is known as an "alligator." So the smart investor stayed away from those house and apartment investments, right? Wrong! It made good sense to feed a $200,000 house $300 or $400 per month if you could sell it two years later for $350,000. No yield. Great growth.

San Francisco Bay Area apartment houses in 1965 were selling for seven times the gross scheduled income (an apartment building with $100,000 per year gross income, selling for $700,000). Because the investor was able to obtain 7% financing, they had good cash flow. In 1975, the same apartment was priced at 8.5 times the gross scheduled income (121% higher price), and the best available loans were at 9%. This combination created an investment that had no cash flow. So, as an investment, this apartment building made no sense at all, right? Certainly, it made no sense from a yield standpoint. But don't tell those who paid $4,000,000 for the apartment, then sold it three years later for $6,000,000, that they made a poor investment. Their bank balance proved otherwise.

As important as growth is, the player must be able to compute and understand yields to effectively play the game. Yields determine what the property will provide in income or cost each month to own. Perhaps more importantly, comparing yields is the primary method to appraise income properties and to determine whether we are purchasing or selling a property at, above, or below the market price.

Most of us are familiar with buying or selling a house. To establish the value of a house, we check out the comparables, the sales and listing prices of similar houses in similar areas. Investment properties—apartments, industrial buildings, shopping centers, office buildings, mobile home parks and self-storage facilities—also require the ability to check out the comparables. But, unlike tract houses, there are very few identical investment properties. We cannot go around a corner and find an identical 47-unit apartment or a 142,798 square foot shopping center anchored by a major chain grocery store. Therefore, we need a common measuring tool to compare properties of different types and sizes—yield. We can compare the yields on all shopping center sales in a community, and reach a determination as to value. The appraiser and knowledgeable investment broker know at what yield a shopping center in San Francisco is an outstanding buy, just as they know when one is overpriced. There are other considerations, such as cost per square foot, or cost per unit, but comparing yields is where we start.

To be an accomplished player, we must be able to compute yields on all types of properties, and then apply that knowledge unemotionally. Chapter 4 is the guide to understanding and computing yields and using those skills to accurately determine true real estate values.

Buying and Selling a Home

Estate building, through real estate investing, is the prime focus of this book. The majority of the population makes only one type of real estate investment in their lifetime—the purchase of their own personal residence. Many investors too, start their wealth-building with a single-family residence.

Because buying a home is a matter of personal taste, no attempt will be made to influence the reader as to appropriate age, size or appearance. However, the home, even while being used as a residence, is still a major investment, often the one that sees the owner through difficult financial times or provides for comfortable retirement years. Many have depended on that investment.

The quality of the investment and the potential for appreciation begins with the purchase.

THE PURCHASE

I have sold homes to people who bought the first house they inspected and on other occasions have driven families around for weeks without them ever buying. It was after three rainy weeks of daily hauling around a couple and their two screaming kids only to have them buy a for-sale-by-owner home that I made the decision to specialize in selling investment properties.

One early lesson learned during my home-selling years was to avoid thinking for my clients. I was taught to pick two or three homes that best matched my prospects' requirements and budget and then show the worst first and the best last. One day I took a couple out and showed them two, three bedroom, two bath homes in the same neighborhood. The first house was a mess. There were holes in the carpet, filthy walls, cabinet doors hanging by one hinge, plumbing fixtures that needed replacing and trash everywhere. The next house had been totally refurbished by the lender-owner. It had been freshly painted inside and out, cabinets re-stained, and new carpet. The two homes were similarly priced.

Standing in the spic-and-span second home, I asked my usual closing question, "Which home do you like?"

The reply was a total shock: "The first home. My kids would just tear this place up anyway. It would be a shame to ruin it."

Yes, home buying is a very individual thing, but most homebuyers also want this very important purchase to be a good investment. Here are several factors to consider.

Location: The homebuyer has less flexibility than an investor as to the location of their purchase. Proximity to work, schools and transportation all help dictate where the homebuyer lives, while an investor is free to consider investments on their own merits anywhere in the world.

The potential resale value of a home will be affected by the city where the home is located as well as the immediate neighborhood. Is the city expanding, or is it in a downward growth spiral? The homebuyer may believe that he or she has no choice as to the city. If one must locate in a specific city, and the city is in a downturn (or poised for one), why buy?

I have a friend, a very successful investor, who owns dozens of homes but does not occupy any of them. He claims, and I agree, that in many parts of the country it is much cheaper to rent than own. The main financial reason to own a home is to take advantage of the home's appreciation. If the potential homebuyer believes there will either be no appreciation, or even a loss, then consider renting. The same funds that were to have been used as a down payment can be better used to acquire an income producing property in a growth area.

Pricing: The cost per square foot of a home will vary with the quality of the home itself and the location. However, it is possible to compare similar homes in the same neighborhood to determine a fair offering price.

In a rapidly increasing pricing market the homebuyer may not be able to acquire the home of choice at the same price as the comparables. This does not mean that the buyer should pass on the home they like. The real estate world is full of woeful tales from potential homebuyers who wouldn't go the extra thousand dollars on the home that shortly was worth thirty thousand above the price they would have paid.

Conversely, in a downward moving market the buyer can, and should, be more of a hard-nosed negotiator. It is likely that if he or she misses out on one home, another will come available at an equal or better price.

Most multiple listing services (MLS) offer the broker the ability to pull up comparables. These should be used as a guideline for home pricing.

The broker: If the homebuyer has an ongoing relationship with a trusted broker, by all means use that broker. If not, a broker who specializes in representing buyers should be considered. Traditionally, sellers pay real estate commissions, and there are usually two agents in each transaction, one representing the buyer, and the listing agent who represents the seller. In the past this led to numerous lawsuits, and ultimately legislation clarified who could do what and be paid by whom.

In California, the seller can pay the entire commission and have one of the agents being paid by that seller actually represent the other party, the buyer. Lengthy purchase agreements and disclosure forms make clear who is representing whom and how everyone is getting paid. The same agent may even act as a dual agent, representing both the buyer and the seller and collecting the entire commission. Given the choice, I believe it makes more sense for the buyer to have their own agent, a buyer's broker. It costs no more, and the buyer's broker's highest duty is to the buyer only. The buyer's broker doesn't care which firm has the property listed. They only want the best deal for their buyer. Unlike the listing broker, discussed later, I believe the small independent often makes the best buyer's broker.

All brokers in large metropolitan areas have access to nearly the same inventory. The MLS database allows the broker to search for properties by nearly any criteria the buyer could imagine. The client who requires a three bedroom, three bath home, between 2,500 and 3,000 square feet, on a quarter acre, with a view of the mountains, in the L.R. Green school district, can be presented with the inventory of those available homes, and their details, within seconds.

Buyers (and sellers) now have many websites to explore. I read somewhere that 85% of all prospective homebuyers begin their search on-line, and that the number will soon reach 95%. Obviously this is a wonderful time saver, especially with virtual tours, Google Earth aerial and street views and Mapquest.

Negotiations: As a buyer's broker, one of my most difficult recommendations is what price my clients should offer for the property of their choice. My duty is to get them the best deal possible, but not lose them the property they are set on owning.

The market condition and competition are the first pricing considerations. Because we usually eliminated the overpriced properties prior to showing, the one the client selects has already been well priced by the listing agent. Suppose we have a home that has been listed at $199,500 and the comparables show that the other two sales for similar homes in the same area were at $205,000 and $208,000. The regional market is weak but firming and I am concerned about competition, as two of my client's other offers (on different properties) have recently been beaten out by other, higher, offers. There are definitely other buyers lurking.

The next pricing consideration is whether my buyers want seller concessions. Do they need, or want, the seller to pay all or part of their closing costs? Do they want some personal property to stay with the home? Does my buyer require some difficult or undesirable seller financing?

Finally, before writing the offer, I call the listing broker to insure the property is still available. I have had numerous experiences where an offer has come in while I was showing the property. This phone call will give me another piece of information to consider in determining the offer. Are there competing offers submitted, or expected? If the listing broker sounds as though my client and I am a savior to himself and his owner, I will suggest a far different offering price than if I know there is another interested party.

As a buyers' broker, in the purchase contract I allow the seller only 24 hours to answer the offer. I do not want our offer being shopped or held awaiting a better one. I always attempt to offer a price low enough that the seller will not immediately agree, but will respond with a counteroffer. However, I do not recommend the price be so low as to make the seller angry and refuse to negotiate. Often, at least three counter-offers are required before the price and terms can be agreed upon.

Once the price and terms are agreed upon, I do not believe either should be changed unless the inspections and disclosures reveal the buyer was misled or not informed about some material defect with the property, documents or financing.

THE SALE:

Just as the best time to purchase a home is during a buyers' market, the best time to sell is during a sellers' market. If the property owner is trapped in a buyers' market and must relocate, keeping the home as a rental until market conditions change is an alternative that must be considered.

Pricing: The market will dictate the price. Only in a rapidly moving-up market can a homeowner expect to receive a price higher than sales of similar homes in the area. Any real estate broker with access to the MLS computer can retrieve the comparables. The seller should carefully check the listing information to insure that the homes being used as comparables are actually comparable. No two existing homes are exactly alike. Is your home in better or worse condition? Have there been additions or upgrades to distinguish your property?

For a home to sell it must be priced realistically. Except to the IRS, it doesn't matter what you paid for the property. A property is worth what a buyer is willing to pay for it. Don't believe you can get more than the market dictates. You can't.

The listing broker: There are many outstanding listing brokers. The best of them will tell you what your property will actually bring. The worst will tell you what you want to hear.

Your listing broker should start by bringing you the comparables. Then he or she should pencil out what you will actually net when the house sells. They will explore your level of motivation, and discuss alternatives. You should get an advertising commitment. Open houses and Internet advertising are now commonplace. Some brokers will place brochures on their signs and others have "talking houses," a recorded advertisement for passersby.

The big residential brokerage houses, Coldwell Banker, Prudential, ERA, Realty Executives, Windermere, Keller-Williams and Century 21, among others, offer the best listing programs. Many top agents work semi-independently under the REMax banner. Interview several, and choose the one that you feel will get the job done and with whom you will enjoy working.

Negotiations: Unless you are selling in a very strong market you will probably never get a full price offer. Expect that. And expect to come down from the listing price, even if only a very small amount. I have known deals to fail just because the sellers were absolutely immovable. The buyer, stubborn too, just said, "To hell with him. We'll find ourselves another place."

There is "face" in negotiations, and buyers must be made to feel they are good negotiators and made the best possible deal. Thus, the seller should never accept the buyer's first offer, even if they are willing to settle for the price and terms offered. If they accept, the buyer will wonder how much lower they should, and could, have gone. A counter-offer, even a few hundred dollars over the original offer, will help insure the buyers' belief that they got the best possible deal.

The remainder of this book is concerned with buying, owning and selling real estate as an investment. As we discussed, your home can be an outstanding investment, too. But a home is much more than that. The majority of one's life is spent in their home, and values far beyond money are reflected there. There is nothing wrong with making the best deal possible, but there is also a lot to be said for living in a wonderful, unique, quirky, strange, different environment that might make little sense financially.

Chapter 4
Analyzing Investment Properties

To be able to consistently and intelligently purchase and sell investment real estate, we must be able to compute and measure yields. Unfortunately, there is a great deal of confusion as to what is meant by "yields." When a prospective investor phones my office and tells me he wants to purchase a property with a 9% yield, I need to ask several questions to determine that person's definition of yield. While the real estate investment brokerage community has developed its own terminology, used worldwide, each investor has his or her own individual definition.

Yield can be (and is) any of the below:
a) The **Capitalization of Net Income** commonly called **Cap Rate;**
b) The **Cash-on-Cash** return;
c) The **Internal Rate of Return** commonly called **IRR;**
d) The **Financial Management Rate of Return** commonly called **FMRR,**
e) The **Return On and Return Of** the investment

The **Cap Rate** computes the return from the property, while **Cash-on-Cash** computes the return on the investment. Both **Cap Rate** and **Cash-on-Cash** measure how the property is doing now.

The **IRR** and the **FMRR** add the ingredient of time. The **Return On and Return Of** the investment computes the recapture of the investment as well as the return on the investment.

The ability to compute Cap Rates and Cash-on-Cash returns is fundamental and needs to be mastered to fully benefit from the remainder of this book. IRRs and FMRRs will be of interest to the more advanced practitioner, and to those who enjoy math and accounting, but the mastery of those concepts is not essential for the investor to be able to make intelligent real estate investment decisions. And IRRs and FMRRs are manipulated by assumptions about growth, which are rarely accurate.

A. CAPITALIZATION OF NET INCOME (CAP RATE)

The first and cornerstone method of measuring real estate yields, the most fundamental of fundamentals, is the **Capitalization of Net Income**, more commonly called the **Cap Rate**.

Whether buying or selling, each property has a PRICE or COST. If it is an income property, it has income. It also has expenses. Sometimes the landlord (owner) pays all of the expenses, and sometimes the tenant pays some or all of the expenses. In business, whatever is left over from the income after the expenses are paid is called profit. In real estate, we call that profit the **Net Operating Income** or **NOI**.

The **Cap Rate** is always expressed as a percentage. It is the percentage of profit the property earns. When computing **Cap Rates** the calculations are made without financing (as if the property were owned free and clear).

Cap Rate FORMULA # 1:

NET OPERATING INCOME divided by PRICE equals **Cap Rate**

EXAMPLE:

An apartment building costs $100,000 and earns a profit of $9,000 per year. $9,000 as a percentage of the $100,000 price is 9%. The property has a 9% cap rate.

$9,000 (NOI/Profit) / $100,000 (Price) = 9% (Cap Rate)

Other things being equal (and they never are),

THE HIGHER THE CAP RATE THE BETTER THE INVESTMENT

NET OPERATING INCOME

In order to obtain the **Cap Rate** we must first know the **Net Operating Income** (**NOI**). The **NOI** is the profit a property earns after expenses are paid (before debt service). The following calculation is used to obtain the **Net Operating Income**:

NET OPERATING INCOME FORMULA
GROSS **SCHEDULED** INCOME (**GSI**)
Less: Vacancy and rent loss
Equals: GROSS **OPERATING** INCOME (**GOI**)
Less: Operating expenses
Equals: NET OPERATING INCOME (**NOI**)

The GROSS **SCHEDULED** INCOME (GSI) is the annual income the property would bring in if it were 100% occupied 100% of the time with all of the tenants always paying all of their rent.

Example: Each unit of a ten unit apartment rents for $700 per month and the laundry room brings in another $200 per month. The monthly rental income from units would be $7,000 per month. $7,000 times 12 equals $84,000 per year scheduled rental income. $200 (the laundry income) times 12 equals $2,400 misc. income. Total GROSS SCHEDULED INCOME equals $84,000 plus $2,400 or $86,400.

Unfortunately for property owners, most properties do not remain 100% occupied 100% of the time, nor do all tenants always pay. Actual income is less than gross scheduled income by the amount of the vacancies and the rent losses incurred when tenants don't pay their rents.

The actual income a property generates is called the GROSS **OPERATING** INCOME.

If we receive an actual operating statement from the owner for the previous year, the income numbers are the GROSS OPERATING INCOME rather than the GROSS SCHEDULED INCOME. If the property owner or broker provides an income projection, that projection will normally show GROSS SCHEDULED INCOME, a vacancy factor, and GROSS OPERATING INCOME.

All apartment buildings, self-storage facilities, and most other investment properties experience vacancies and rent losses. The exception is the single tenant building with a very strong tenant (i.e. credit tenant) on a long-term lease. The U.S. Post Office, McDonalds and Google are credit tenant examples.

The final step in calculating NET OPERATING INCOME is to subtract OPERATING EXPENSES from GROSS OPERATING INCOME.
Operating expenses include:
Property Taxes
Insurance
Management (on and/or off site)
Maintenance & Repairs
Supplies
Utilities (electricity, gas, water, garbage, sewer, phone)
Gardening
Legal and Accounting
Services (janitorial, pool, window washing, pest control, elevator, lot sweeping)
Miscellaneous

Do NOT include book depreciation (see chapter on tax shelters) and interest payments, including interest on loans. Interest is a function of financing and book depreciation is computed for tax purposes. An actual reserve, funds set aside, for replacement of depreciable items should be included as an expense item. Most operating statements prepared by accountants will have both depreciation and interest included as expense items. These must be removed to obtain the applicable operating expenses.

Projected operating expenses is one of the most abused areas in preparing real estate investment proformas (projections of future income and expenses), especially when dealing with apartments and other small investment properties. Owners and newer investment brokers tend to underestimate operating expenses. I have heard owner's property proformas referred to as "The Big Lie." All properties have taxes, insurance and management. All improved properties have maintenance, repairs and utility costs. Only in the case of triple net leases, where the tenant pays all expenses, does the property owner escape these expenses.

There are some rules of thumb in estimating expenses. In apartments where tenants pay their own utilities, expenses will usually run a minimum of 25% of the gross operating income PLUS the property taxes. The investor should be aware that property taxes may increase upon the property being transferred to a new buyer.

Now that we have covered all the steps necessary to compute **Net Operating Income**, we will further clarify the process with an example.

EXAMPLE: An apartment building has annual GROSS SCHEDULED INCOME of $86,400, a 5% vacancy and rent loss, and $29,976 in annual expenses.

What is the NET OPERATING INCOME?

GROSS SCHEDULED INCOME	$86,400
Less: vacancy & rent loss (5%)	(-) 4,320
Equals: GROSS OPERATING INCOME	$82,080
Less: operating expenses	$29,976
Equals: NET OPERATING INCOME (NOI)	$52,104

If the building could be purchased for $580,000 it would have a **Cap Rate** of 8.98%

CAP RATE FORMULA:

$52,104 (NOI) / $580,000 (Price) = 8.98% (Cap Rate)

Decades ago, before computers and spreadsheets, the Certified Commercial Investment Member (CCIM) and the investment real estate community at large created various forms, A through E, to compute cap rate, cash on cash returns, IRRs and FMRRs. My earlier book and seminars instructed students in filling out a Form A. Now we have Excel. For readers who are unfamiliar with Excel, I recommend you find a tutorial and learn the basics.

When I was studying to become a CCIM, the examiners were just discovering IRRs (Internal Rate of Return) and it was becoming the darling of CCIM philosophy. Unfortunately, at that time, the only way to compute an Internal Rate of Return was to consult the Ellwood Tables, a book of computations and numbers the student would apply to cash flows, appreciation, time and sales pricing. To solve a simple IRR problem using the Ellwood tables was a day-long task. Now, an Excel formula will spit out an IRR in seconds.

I have created an Excel spreadsheet to use to compute Cap Rates and Cash-on-Cash Returns. The blank form that follows can be replicated on your computer. The cells for rental income can be changed to fit commercial, office, industrial or self- storage tenants. If the property has more than the six tenant types provided, simply add more rows. The same is true with expenses.

Property Analysis Form A

Property Information	Name/ Address				
Price		# Units		Price / Unit	
Total Loans		Sq Ft		Price / Ft	
Down Payment		Closing		Investment	
	#	Average	Total	Actual	Projected
Income	of	Monthly	Monthly	Annual	Income &
Unit Mix / Tenant	Units	Rent	Income	Rent	Expenses
					-
Other & Misc					
Gross Scheduled Income					
Vacancy & Rent Loss					
Gross Operating Income					
Expenses				Annual	
Property Taxes					
Insurance					
Management On-site					
Management Off-site					
Maintenance & Repairs					
Supplies					
Utilities					
Gardening & Pool					
Legal & Accounting					
Advertising					
Travel					
Services (pool, pest, etc)					
Miscellaneous					
Total Annual Expenses				-	-
Expenses as % of GOI					
Net Operating Income					
Cap Rate					
Loan Payments	Monthly		Annual		
Cash Flow					
Cash on Cash Return					

As you can see, the top portion has cells for general information about the property including price, total loans, closing costs, equity, location, and square footage. If the property is an apartment building, self-storage facility, hotel or motel, there is a cell for number of units. By dividing the price by the square footage and number of units we can determine the price per square foot and price per unit. This is very helpful in comparing prices of similar properties.

On the left side of the top section is a place for the price and total financing, existing or available. By subtracting the financing from the price we arrive at the equity or down payment. The down payment plus the closing costs equals the initial cash investment. Below this property information is a section labeled "Income" which provides cells to enter rental information.

In the case of a ten unit apartment complex, the following entry would be made:

	Actual	
Unit Mix / Tenant	Av Monthly Rent	# of Units
1 Bdrm 1 Ba	500	2
2 Bdrm 1 Ba	675	4
3 Bdrm 2 Ba	850	4
Misc.	100	1

A three tenant industrial building might be entered as follows:

	Actual	
Unit Mix / Tenant	Av Monthly Rent	# of Units
Fix-it Auto	2,700	1
Bob's Construction	3,100	1
Dan's Cabinets	4,200	1
Misc.	100	1

Let's walk through the information needed to complete the Property Analysis Form A for a ten unit apartment building with a laundry room (categorized as misc).

Property Name/ Address: Front Street Apts.; 123 Front St, Sacramento, CA; **# of Units**: 10
Price: $580,000; **Total Loans:** $435,000; **Square Feet:** 8,800; **Closing:** $5,800

Income:	Actual	
Unit Mix / Tenant	Av Monthly Rent	# of Units
1 Bdrm 1 Ba	500	2
2 Bdrm 1 Ba	675	4
3 Bdrm 2 Ba	850	4
Misc.	100	1

The monthly rents are totaled and multiplied by 12 to obtain the annual **Gross Scheduled Income.**

Vacancy and Rent Loss: The Form A has cells for both the actual and projected vacancy. Both are very important. An apartment building 50% vacant selling at an 8% cap rate, based on actual income, offers a great deal of upside profit potential if the vacancies can be filled. Conversely, an industrial building 95% full has a huge downside if a major tenant's lease is about to expire and their lease renewal is unsecured.

The Gross Scheduled Income (GSI) less the vacancy and Rent Loss becomes the **Gross Operating Income** (the property's actual annual income).

Expenses: Below the income section is the operating expenses section. Monthly expenses should be annualized to complete this column.

Property Taxes:	$5,800 (1% of the sales price)
Insurance:	$2,000
On site management:	$200 per month
Off site management:	$3,876
Maintenance & repair:	$3,000
Supplies:	$1,000
Utilities:	$4,500
Advertising:	$600

Gardener and pool service: $300 per month
Pest control contract: $100 per month
Legal and accounting: $1,200
Miscellaneous: $800

Now we can complete a sample PROPERTY ANALYSIS FORM A with the information provided. Cells requiring a formula are numbered, and the formulas provided below the spreadsheet sample.

Preparer fills in the following:

1) Property name/address;
2) Price;
3) Total Loans;
4) Square footage;
5) Unit Mix or Tenant List

6) Number of Units of Each Type
7) Average Monthly Rents
8) Breakdown of Actual Expenses
9) Total Annual Loan Payment

Property Information	Name/ Address		Front St. Apts, 123 Front St, Sacramento CA	
Price	580,000	**# Units** 10	**Price / Unit**	[2]
Total Loans	435,000	**Sq Ft** 8,800	**Price / Ft**	[3]
Equity	[1]	**Closing** 5,800	**Investment**	[4]
	#	Average	Total	Actual	Projected
Income	**of**	**Monthly**	**Monthly**	**Annual**	**Income &**
Unit Mix / Tenant	**Units**	**Rent**	**Income**	**Rent**	**Expenses**
1 Bdrm 1 Ba	2	500	[5]	[6]	
2 Bdrm 2 Ba	4	675	[5]	[6]	-
3 Bdrm 2 Ba	4	850	[5]	[6]	
Other & Misc	1	100	[5]	[6]	
Gross Scheduled Income			[7]	[8]	[8]
Vacancy & Rent Loss					
Gross Operating Income				[9]	[9]
Expenses				**Annual**	
Property Taxes				5,800	
Insurance				2,000	
Management On-site				2,400	
Management Off-site				3,876	
Maintenance & Repairs				3,000	
Supplies				1,000	
Utilities				4,500	
Gardening & Pool				3,600	

Legal & Accounting				1,200	
Advertising				600	
Services (pool, pest, etc)				1,200	
Miscellaneous				800	
Total Annual Expenses				[10]	[10]
Expenses as % of GOI	[11]				
Net Operating Income				[12]	[12]
Cap Rate				[13]	[13]
Loan Payments	Monthly	2,894.07	X 12 =	34,729	
Cash Flow				[14]	[14]
Cash on Cash Return				[15]	[15]

Formulas (let Excel do this work for you):

[1] Equity = Price – Total Loans   (=580,000-435,000)   Result: $145,000

[2] Price / Unit = Price / # Units   (=580,000/10)   Result: $58,000

[3] Price / Foot = Price / Sq Ft   (=580,000/8800)   Result: $49.43

[4] Investment = Equity + Closing   (=145,000+5,800)   Result: $150,800

[5] Monthly Income = # of unit type *Avg Rent Monthly (=4*675) Result= $2,700

[6] Annual Income = Monthly Income * 12 (=2,700*12)   Result: $32,400

[7] Scheduled Monthly Income =[5]+[5]+[5]+[5]   Result: $7,200

[8] Scheduled Annual Income =[6]+[6]+[6]+[6]   Result: $86,400

The form has a column for Projected Income and Expenses. This is a common computation, especially for apartment buildings, as there are thousands of projects across the country with vacancies exceeding 50%, and most owner/sellers will say that the complex is under-rented.

Another typical owner/seller claim is that they could get higher unit rents, but the existing tenants have lived there so long and are so loyal that they didn't have the heart to increase the rents to present day comparables. The completed spreadsheet will show a higher projected NOI and Cap Rate to reflect our projected rent increases: new monthly one bedroom rents of $550, monthly two bedroom rents of $700 and monthly three bedroom rents of $900. Projected annual rental income totals of $13,200, $33,600, & $43,200 per unit type, combined with $1,200 in annual projected laundry income, result in a projected GSI of $91,200.

The same formulas are used to compute both the actual income and projected income, expenses, NOI, cap rates and cash-on-cash returns.

[9] Gross Operating Income = GSI – vacancy / rent loss (=86,400-4,320)   Result $82,080
[10] Total Annual Expenses = taxes + insurance + + + (=5,500 + + +)   Result 29,976
[11] Expense Percentage = Total Expenses / GOI (=29,976/82,080)   Result $36.5%
[12] Net Operating Income = GOI - total expenses (=82,080-29,976)   Result $52,104
[13] Cap Rate = NOI/Price (=52,104/580,000)   Result 8.983%
[14] Cash Flow = NOI - total loan payments (=52.104-34,729)   Result $17,375
[15] Cash-on-Cash Return = Cash Flow / Investment (=17,375/150,800)   Result 11.52%

See Results following:

Property Analysis Form A

Property Information	Name / Address		Front Street Apts, 123 Front St, Sacramento		
Price	580,000	# Units	10	Price / Unit	58,000
Total Loans	435,000	Sq Ft	8,800	Price / Ft	49.43
Down Payment	145,000	Closing	5,800	Investment	150,800
	#	Average	Total	Actual	Projected
Income	of	Monthly	Monthly	Annual	Income &
Unit Mix / Tenants	Units	Rent	Income	Rent	Expenses
1 Bdrm 1 Ba	2	500	1,000	12,000	13,200
2 Bdrm 2 Ba	4	675	2,700	32,400	33,600
3 Bdrm 2 Ba	4	850	3,400	40,800	43,200
Other & Misc	1	100	100	1,200	1,200
Gross Scheduled Income			7,200	86,400	91,200
Vacancy & Rent Loss				4,320	4,560
Gross Operating Income				82,080	86,640
Expenses				Annual	
Property Taxes				5,800	
Insurance				2,000	
Management On-site				2,400	
Management Off-site				3,876	
Maintenance & Repairs				3,000	
Supplies				1,000	
Utilities				4,500	
Gardening & Pool				3,600	
Legal & Accounting				1,200	
Advertising				600	
Travel				-	
Services (pool, pest, etc)				1,200	

Miscellaneous					800	
Total Annual Expenses					29,976	29,976
Expenses as % of GOI	36.52%					
Net Operating Income					**52,104**	**56,664**
Cap Rate					**8.983%**	**9.770%**
Loan Payments	Monthly	2,894.07	X 12 =		34,729	34,729
Cash Flow					**17,375**	**21,935**
Cash on Cash Return					**11.522%**	**14.546%**

Summary ANALYSIS	
GROSS SCHEDULED INCOME	86,400
Less: VACANCY & RENT LOSS (5%)	4,320
Equals: GROSS OPERATING INCOME	82,080
Less: OPERATING EXPENSES	29,976
Equals: NET OPERATING INCOME	52,104
CAP RATE	8.98%

Whether this property is a good buy at an 8.98% CAP RATE will depend on the comparables in the area and the market conditions at the time. CAP RATES on properties throughout the United States vary widely. Apartment buildings in San Francisco, La Jolla and Newport Beach, California will usually sell with cap rates lower than 7%; high-risk commercial properties in some Midwestern cities will sell with cap rates of 13% and higher.

Excluding houses, apartment buildings usually have the lowest CAP RATES of any investment properties, while commercial, industrial, and self-storage properties tend to have higher cap rates. Properties in California tend to have lower CAP RATES than those in Kansas, Indiana or Mississippi.

We will return to Form A momentarily to compute CASH-ON-CASH returns.

First, let's review an alternative CAP RATE formula useful in investment analysis. It's a variation of the original cap rate formula, used when we know the NET OPERATING INCOME and we need to determine what price will meet the client's guidelines for purchasing the property.

Cap Rate FORMULA #2:
NET OPERATING INCOME divided by CAP RATE equals PRICE

EXAMPLE:
We have a client who will purchase a commercial shopping center provided it has at least a 9% cap rate. A property is available with an annual **Net Operating Income** of $500,000. At what price would our client purchase this shopping center?

$500,000 (NOI) / .09 (Cap Rate) = $5,555,555 (Price)

B. CASH-ON-CASH

While the cornerstone of all investment analysis is an understanding of CAP RATES, many investors are more interested in the CASH-ON-CASH return. Comparing CAP RATES is the most objective method of comparing a property's yield. However, comparing cap rates is not necessarily the best method of evaluating the investment.

CASH-ON-CASH is the method used to measure the return on the investment. How the investment performs is dependent on how the property performs (CAP RATE) but it is also dependent on the financing.

CASH-ON-CASH is the annual percentage of cash return on the cash investment. For instance, when we place $10,000 in the bank and receive $600 in interest at the end of the year, we have received 6% cash return on cash invested.

The following three step formula is used to compute CASH-ON-CASH:

CASH-ON-CASH FORMULA # 1

STEP 1:

NET OPERATING INCOME less Annual Loan Payments equals CASH FLOW

STEP 2:

DOWN PAYMENT plus Closing Costs equals CASH INVESTED

STEP 3:

CASH FLOW divided by CASH INVESTED equals CASH-ON-CASH return

EXAMPLE: A property offered at a price of $100,000 has a $75,000 loan, requiring a down payment of $25,000. Buyer's closing costs are $5,000. The property has a NET OPERATING INCOME OF $9,500 per year and a loan payment of $7,500 per year.

Step 1: $9,500 (NOI) - $7,500 (Loan Payments) = $2,000 (Cash Flow)

Step 2: $25,000 (Down Payment) + $5,000 (Closing Costs) = $30,000 (Cash Invested)

Step 3: $2,000 (Cash Flow) / $30,000 (Cash Invested) = $6.67% (Cash-on-Cash return, expressed as a percentage)

Returning to the ten-unit apartment example, we can use the information from our Property Analysis Form A, as well as the financing terms provided below, to assist in our calculation of the cash-on-cash return. The property had a $435,000 loan, payable at $2,894.07 per month, including interest at 7% per annum. In this example, there is only one loan, so the annual payment on the first loan, and the total of all loan payments on this property, is $34,729 ($2,894.07*12).

Step 1: $52,104 (NOI) - $34,729 (Loan Payments) = $17,375 (Cash Flow)

Step 2: $145,000 (Down Payment) + $5,800 (Closing Costs) = $150,800 (Cash Invested)

Step 3: $17,375 (Cash Flow) / $150,800 (Cash Invested) = 11.522% (Cash-on-Cash return)

As with the cap rate, the higher the better...

There is another investment formula that utilizes CASH-ON-CASH. This formula is used when we know the CASH FLOW and the Buyer's CASH-ON-CASH requirements and we need to determine what price the Buyer will pay for the property. This is a two step formula.

CASH-ON-CASH FORMULA # 2:
STEP 1:
CASH FLOW divided by CASH-ON-CASH REQUIRED equals INVESTMENT

STEP 2:
INVESTMENT
(-) CLOSING COSTS
(+) LOANS
(=) PRICE

EXAMPLE: An investor has a maximum of $1,500,000 to invest and he/she requires a minimum 5% first-year CASH-ON-CASH return. A shopping center comes on the market priced at $2,500,000 with a $1,500,000 loan. The cash flow is $50,000 per year and buyer's closing costs are estimated at $35,000. How much will the investor pay for the property?

STEP I: $50,000 (Cash Flow) / .05 (Cash-on-Cash return) = $1,000,000 (Investment)

STEP 2
CASH INVESTED	1,000,000
(-) CLOSING COSTS	35,000
(+) LOANS	1,500,000
(=) PRICE	2,465,000

The investor will pay $2,465,000

C. INTERNAL RATE OF RETURN (IRR) and Financial Management Rates of Return (FMRR)

Cap Rates and Cash-on-Cash returns do not address the time value of money. They merely tell the investor how the property is performing NOW. But, the investor does not receive the return on the investment NOW. Some dollars come in (or go out) each month, hopefully more arriving in future years, and eventually a very large, one-time payment will be received from the sale of the property, with possibly some later payments coming in if there is an installment sale (loan carried back by seller with periodic payments).

The sophisticated investor must take the position that the money received at some future date has less value than if the funds were received today. The money could be invested if we had it now, which would earn more money for us by that future date.

Through the use of a hand-held financial computer or a spreadsheet, the investor or investment broker can determine the present annual value of the future income stream (periodic receipt of income receipt). This is called the Internal Rate of Return (IRR). The following is an example of an IRR.

EXAMPLE: An investor invests $1,000,000 in an office building. The first year of ownership the building returns a cash flow of $2,000; year two it returns $50,000; year three $100,000; year four it loses $20,000, year five it returns $150,000; and, in year six, it sells, netting the investor (after commissions, loan payoff and closing costs) $1,800,000. What is the annual return on the investment (IRR)? Using an Excel spreadsheet and formula, the following calculation is made.

Investment	(1,000,000)
Year 1	2,000
Year 2	50,000
Year 3	100,000
Year 4	(20,000)
Year 5	150,000
Year 6	1,800,000
	13.87%

Formula is: =IRR(B1:B7)

The annual return on this investment (IRR) over the six years is 13.87%.

Until the 1970s, brokers didn't compute IRRs. It was too much work. We had to use tables and do the math calculations on one year at a time. The small example above, which I did in about 30 seconds in Excel, would have taken hours. Now IRRs are an everyday tool of the more advanced investment broker.

The Financial Management Rate of Return (FMRR) is similar to the IRR except it is more sophisticated. The yield on the income stream is computed and then the cash that may be needed to cover a shortfall and the funds from the income stream itself are given a "safe" return percentage, and these returns are added into the computations. Confused? Most people are, and I will spend no more time on FMRRs.

IRRs and FMRRs are valuable tools for comparing investment alternatives, but there is one glaring weakness in their nature. No one can predict the future and the IRR and FMRR percentages are based on assumptions of future happenings—annual increases in property values and future rents. Your calculations can point to a great investment property with an eight percent annual increase in value, but they are merely conjecture. No one can tell you that it will have that eight percent annual appreciation.

Personally, I am very suspect of IRRs and FMRRs. By combining high leverage (a low down payment and a big loan) with high annual growth projections, I can manipulate the numbers to show an investor great IRR or FMRR percentage returns, regardless of the real value of the properties. CAP RATES and CASH-ON-CASH returns in similar geographical areas are a more valid (less speculative) measurement of comparative property values.

D. RETURN OF AND RETURN ON THE INVESTMENT

When dealing in properties that are potentially obsolete at the expiration of a lease, many investors are not only concerned about the return on the investment (CAP RATE or CASH-ON-CASH), but the return of (the recovery of) the investment.

Suppose a major supermarket has ten years remaining on their lease of an 18,000 square foot store. All of their new stores are 24,000 square feet and designed so their products can be handled by forklift. It must be anticipated that at the expiration of the lease, the major supermarket will vacate, and either the store will remain vacant or it will be rented to another, potentially weaker, tenant at a different rental amount. It is conceivable that the economics will dictate that the old store be torn down and a new one constructed to accommodate the major supermarket.

A sophisticated investor may not only want a return on the investment, but a return of the investment. Typically, the investor does not expect a return **of** the investment in the land portion, as the land normally will not lose its value. But, the investor may want all, or a portion of the investment in the improvements returned over the period of the lease.

Example: A major supermarket pays rent of $50,000 per year. This income stream is valued at a 9% CAP RATE, or $666,667 ($50,000/9%=$666,667). The land is valued at $350,000. An investor may take the position that he/she will pay $350,000 for the land (and its 9% lease portion return) but, in addition to the supermarket lease's 9% return, wants the recovery of his/her anticipated annual 10% investment in maintaining and improving the building over the next ten years. After all, the building may be worth nothing at the end of ten years. Therefore, the investor would expect a 19% return on the property (10% annual return of the investment plus 9% annual return on the investment). Allotting $31,500 ($350,000 x 9%) of the $50,000 income stream to the 9% return on the land, the remaining income of $18,500 ($50,000 total income less $31,500 land return) is available for the return on (9%) and return of the building investment. Dividing the 18,500 by 19%, the investor would then be willing to pay $97,368 for the building (plus the $350,000 for the land) or $447,368 for the entire property.

The investor becomes concerned with the return of and return on the investment when amortizing (paying off over a period of time) the cost of tenant improvements. A tenant willing to sign only a five year lease and requiring $100,000 in tenant improvements may expect the rental rate to reflect the property owner's recovery of the $100,000 expenditure over the five year period, as well as a return on that amount.

Return of the investment is also critical when dealing with purchasing a building on leased land if the building ownership transfers to the land owner at the end of the lease period.

Most investors do not concern themselves with return **of** real estate investments because historically real estate, both land and improvements, has appreciated. Therefore investors recover their investment, and more, upon sale.

To review the distinctions between various measurable yields, CAP RATES are the most accurate measurement of a property's value, NOW. CASH-ON-CASH returns are the most accurate measurement of an investment, NOW. IRRs and FMRRs have a value in investment analysis, but their numbers can be easily manipulated since they are predictive, based on the unknowable future. The return of (in addition to the return on) an investment must be considered when investing in properties on leased land; properties becoming obsolete; and when dealing with tenant improvements.

Chapter 5
Financing Investment Real Estate

Very few investors pay all cash for real estate, so most real estate investments require financing. Real estate financing falls into three major categories— institutional financing, private money lenders, and owner carry-back.

INSTITUTIONAL FINANCING

Institutional financing is the primary source of real property financing. Real estate loans are secured by the real estate. That means the lender has the right to foreclose on the real estate pledged as security if the borrower fails to make the loan payments as agreed. Generally the institutional lender demands to be in first position. First position assures the institution they will receive a priority on the return of their money, before any other creditors.

SECURITY INSTRUMENTS

The borrower of a real estate loan gives the lender a promissory note and also executes the security document, which makes the loan a secured loan. Depending on the state, the security instrument will either be a mortgage or a trust deed.

A mortgage document has two parties, the mortgagor (the person who borrows against his/her property) and the mortgagee (the lender). The mortgage will contain the legal language regarding default and the rights of the parties.

The trust deed is the security instrument used in California and many other states. There are three parties to a trust deed; the trustor (the borrower), the beneficiary (the lender), and the trustee (the neutral party who holds the document and will act on behalf of the beneficiary if the trustor doesn't make the loan payments as agreed). The trust deed, like the mortgage, contains the legal language and the rights of the parties.

LENDER FEES AND CHARGES

Lenders obtain their income from several sources, the two most important of which are INTEREST and POINTS.

INTEREST is the ongoing charge for the use of the lender's money. The INTEREST charge is usually quoted as the annual interest rate. For example, 10% interest usually means the charge for the use of the money is 10% of the loan balance for a year's use of the money.

Interest rates can be fixed, variable or a combination thereof. If the loan has a variable interest rate, it is usually tied to an index. Examples of indexes include: Prime; 10 year treasuries; A district cost of funds; and LIBOR.

Typically, the borrower is better off with a fixed interest rate loan if interest rates are rising and with a variable rate loan if they are falling. Many variable loans have "teaser" rates; a lower start rate that helps the buyer qualify and assists the buyer during early periods of ownership.

POINTS are a one-time charge for placing the loan. One point is one percent. A two point loan fee on a $100,000 loan would be $2,000.

Lenders also charge fees for loan assumptions (a new buyer taking over the old owner's loan), and loan prepayments (if a borrower pays off a loan early). Many loans now have "lock-in" clauses that prohibit the loan being prepaid.

Before committing to a lender, the investor should thoroughly investigate each potential lender's rates and policies regarding assumptions, lock-ins and prepayments.

LOAN-TO-VALUE RATIOS and DEBT-COVERAGE RATIOS:

The loan-to-value ratio is the amount the lender will lend as a ratio of a property's value. As an example, a lender who will make a 75% loan will loan $75,000 on a building they appraise at $100,000. If a lender's maximum loan percentage is 75%, their maximum loan will generally be 75% of the appraisal or sales price, whichever is LESS.

Additionally, lenders want to ensure that an income property can service the loan. So, most require that the Net Operating Income be in excess of the annual loan payments by a certain percentage. Common debt-coverage ratios include 1.20, 1.25 and 1.30. A debt-coverage ratio of 1.25 on a property with a Net Operating Income of $100,000 would require that the annual loan payments not exceed $80,000($100,000/1.25=$80,000). This may restrict the loan amount to less than the 75% loan-to-value ratio otherwise permitted.

Maximum loan-to-value ratios for institutional lenders are determined by bank and Savings and Loan regulators. Many lenders will set their own ratios at less than the maximum allowed by the regulators. The following is a partial list of the maximum loan-to-value ratios currently permissible:

- Houses   75-95%
- Condominiums   75-95%
- Apartments   75-80%
- Commercial   75%
- Industrial   75%
- Completed lots   0-50%
- Land   0-50%

TYPES OF INSTITUTIONAL LOANS

PERMANENT LOANS

By far the most common institutional real estate loan is the PERMA-NENT LOAN. This is the type of loan most of us have used to finance our homes, and it is the one used as the primary loan on most investment properties. Commonly it is called a "first mortgage" or "first trust deed," as it is in first position amongst creditors. When dealing with new construction, this loan would replace the construction loan and would be called the "take-out loan."

The duration of a permanent loan may be three to forty years. These loans may have a fixed or adjustable interest rate. An adjustable rate loan is sometimes called an ARM, for Adjustable Rate Mortgage. ARMs commonly have a "ceiling" and a "floor": the interest rate can go no higher than the ceiling and it can go no lower than the floor. Typically the rate cannot adjust more often than every three or six months. Fixed rate loans may have rate adjustments every three or five years.

Loans can be FULLY AMORTIZING, INTEREST ONLY, PARTIALLY AMORTIZING, or ACCRUING.

The payments on an FULLY AMORTIZING LOAN include interest and principle and are designed to pay the loan down to zero over the loan period. For example, monthly payments of $877.57 will pay off a $100,000, 10% interest loan over thirty years.

On an INTEREST ONLY loan, the borrower makes no payments on the loan principal. Monthly, quarterly, semi-annual or annual payments are made, but only on the interest owed. This type of loan has a DUE DATE. On that date, the entire principal balance is due and payable. A typical INTEREST ONLY loan would have a due date of one to five years. Occasionally an INTEREST ONLY loan will be written with a 10 to 12 year due date.

A PARTIALLY AMORTIZING loan is a hybrid. The loan payments are set up as though the loan were fully amortizing, typically over 25 or 30 years. However, this loan has a DUE DATE, at which time the remaining principal balance is due and payable. As an example, if the $100,000 loan with $877.57 monthly payments mentioned above had a ten year DUE DATE, the principal amount due at the end of ten years would be $90,938.02.

An ACCRUAL loan also has a DUE DATE. The payments on an ACCRUAL loan are not sufficient to pay the loan interest. Therefore, the principle loan balance GROWS. For example, a $100,000 loan at 10% interest generates annual loan interest of $10,000. Under an accrual loan, the annual loan payments may only be $5,000, with the balance of the interest amount accruing each year. When the due date arrives, the principal balance will be $5,000 higher for each year of the life of the loan.

CONSTRUCTION LOANS:
Builders and owners use CONSTRUCTION LOANS for the funds to build projects. CONSTRUCTION LOANS are usually short-term, interest only loans. Typically, the loan term is determined by the time that it will take to complete the project. A loan to construct a house would typically have a six month to one year term. A major high-rise office building might require a three year CONSTRUCTION LOAN.

The interest rates on construction loans "float," they go up and down with an index, such as the prime rate. Because my building companies are of medium strength, my construction loans usually are at two percent over prime and I typically pay a loan fee of 1 1/2 to two points.

LAND ACQUISITION LOANS:
This loan is used to finance the acquisition of land. Many banks and Savings and Loan Associations will not make this kind of loan, leaving this lending to mortgage companies, private lenders and the few agreeable banks and S&Ls. Typically, the best available loan-to-value ratio is 50% and land acquisition loans are subject to higher than normal interest rates.

DEVELOPMENT LOANS:

A development loan is used to construct the off-site improvements (the streets, curbs, gutters, and sewer, water, gas and electric lines). If the land is owned free and clear, a lender will often make a loan equal to 100% of these costs. The borrower can expect to pay 1 1/2 to three points and have an interest rate of 1 ½% to 3% over prime.

ACQUISITION AND DEVELOPMENT (A&D) LOANS:

This is the type of loan that developers obtain to acquire and subdivide land. The lender appraises the finished lots and then commits to an amount equal to its loan-to-value percentage, usually 70-75%. These loans float at 1 1/2 to three over prime and carry a charge of 1 1/2 to three points.

PARTICIPATION LOANS:

Occasionally, if a borrower needs a loan amount greater than the lender's loan-to-value ratio will permit, the lender may agree to advance additional financing, provided the borrower agrees to pay the lender a share of the expected profits from the project. This is called a participation loan, also referred to by the slang term "a kicker." For example, if the lender typically makes a 75% loan and the borrower needs 85%, the lender may ask a 20% kicker (wants 20% of the profits) in return for the additional 10% financing. If the borrower requires a loan equal to 100% of the costs, the lender may require 50% participation. This makes the project a joint venture.

LOAN COMMITMENT

The loan commitment is the document the lender gives to the borrower (for a fee) that commits the lender to make the loan.

STANDBY COMMITMENT:

Often a builder-borrower gets caught in a situation where a construction lender will not make a construction loan without the borrower having a take-out (permanent) loan committed, thus ensuring that, upon completion, the construction loan can be paid off from the proceeds of the take-out loan. The problem is that many permanent lenders will not place, or commit to a loan until the project is complete and rented to a stipulated occupancy. Thus was born the standby commitment. This is a commitment to make a permanent loan by a lender who never expects to make that loan. For one or two points, prior to commencement of construction, a lender in the business of making standby commitments will commit to make a permanent loan at an above market interest rate and above market points. The borrower does not expect to use this loan. Instead the borrower expects, upon completion and rent-up, to obtain an at market loan from one of the lenders who would not make the permanent loan prior to construction. The one or two points paid for the standby commitment is usually an additional expense of construction which is unnecessary if the market permanent loan is available in advance.

SECONDARY FINANCING: (Mezzanine or Mez Loans)
Most institutional lenders for major investment properties require their financing to be in the first or primary position (i.e., secured by a first mortgage or first trust deed). Some lenders will also make junior loans: in case of foreclosure, the primary, or senior, loan gets paid off and only if sufficient funds are available will the junior loans get paid. These are called "seconds" (or, if even more junior, thirds, fourths, etc.), which is short for second mortgages or second trust deeds. As these loans are in a higher risk position, they command higher interest rates and greater points.

TYPES OF INSTITUTIONAL LENDERS

BANKS:
Banks make permanent real estate loans of all sizes and of all types. Their rates are competitive and their lending limits (loan-to-value ratios) regulated. Large banks have real estate loan departments. The local branch can either take the loan application or refer the borrower to the appropriate party.

SAVINGS AND LOAN ASSOCIATIONS (SAVINGS BANKS, THRIFTS):
These institutions were founded to make real estate loans. They are able to make the same types of loans as banks, except they are not in the business of making personal unsecured loans or setting up lines of credit.

INSURANCE COMPANIES:
Insurance companies make large permanent loans on investment properties such as office buildings and shopping centers. The loans with these institutions are usually arranged by loan correspondents, an independent mortgage broker who has a contract with the insurance company to represent it by placing funds into real estate loans. The rates charged by the insurance companies can be quite competitive, and the loan fee to the correspondent is reasonable (one to two points).

MORTGAGE COMPANIES:
A full service real estate mortgage company is able to provide the borrower with a variety of loans and can handle nearly all of a borrower's real estate loan needs. Most handle government insured home loans (FHA, VA), many are correspondents for life insurance companies, and most are familiar with the kinds of loans available from various banks and savings and loan associations. The mortgage company is also a source for private lenders. For typical institutional financing, the mortgage company will usually charge a one point fee for their services. This is in addition to whatever fees the actual lender (bank, S&L, life insurance company) charges. For private lender loans, the fees are substantially higher.

PRIVATE MONEY LENDERS
Private money lenders are a second source of funds. Many individuals with investment funds regularly make real estate loans. This is often the best source for the unusual or difficult loan. I regularly use private money lenders for land loans, seconds and for unsecured loans for my development equity capital. Many private lenders deal directly with

borrowers while others work through mortgage brokers. As a mortgage broker may charge six to ten points to broker private lender funds, I normally attempt to deal directly with this type of lender. An ad in the newspaper is one method used to locate private lenders. The best way I have found is to work through my accountant. He usually has clients looking for a better than average investment return, and we are able to obtain private money financing at a reasonable rate, with no points. It is very beneficial for both borrower and lender as there is no middle man.

SELLER FINANCING

A third source of real estate financing is seller financing. When the seller does not require all cash from the sale of the property and the property buyer does not have sufficient funds for a normal down payment (the difference between the institutional first loan and the sales price), it is not unusual for the buyer to ask the seller to carry back (lend the buyer/borrower) the shortfall. Example: Purchase price, $100,000; institutional first loan, $75,000; buyer cash, $15,000; buyer asks seller to carry-back a $10,000 loan secured by a note and second trust deed (or mortgage) against the property.

TYPES OF JUNIOR LOANS

THE SELLER CARRY-BACK SECOND:

The typical seller carry-back second is either fully amortizing or interest only. The term is negotiable, but three to five years is quite common. Seller carry-back seconds will often have an interest rate at or below the interest rate on the institutional first loan, as this is often one of the inducements the seller will use to encourage the buyer to purchase the property. I have never heard of points being charged on a seller carry-back loan.

HARD MONEY SECONDS:

This is the type of second usually obtained through a mortgage broker. The interest rates will often be three to five percent greater than on an institutional first loan and the mortgage broker may charge ten points or more.

SLEEPING SECONDS:

Often properties will not show the cash-on-cash returns required by the buyer with the buyer making payments on both the first and second loans. As an incentive, a motivated seller might agree to carrying back a second that has no payments for a period of years. This is called a "sleeping second." Owner carry-back seconds can be structured in any manner agreeable to both parties, and often the seller must make concessions to market difficult to sell properties.

CONSTANTS:

"Constant," short for constant annual percentage, is one of the handiest tools in investment real estate because there is a direct relationship between loan constants and cash-on-cash returns. Simply, constant is the sum of all principal and interest payments (required in the course of the year by the lenders) expressed as a percentage of the amount owing on the loan(s).

CONSTANT FORMULA:

Total Annual Loan Payments divided by the Total Amount of Loan(s) equals The Constant Annual Percentage ("Constant")

For example, if we borrow $100,000 at 10% interest with loan payments totaling $11,000 per year, the constant would be 11%.

$11,000 (Annual Loan Payments) / $100,000 (Total Loan) = 11% (Constant, expressed as a percentage)

The most difficult part of computing constants might be determining the monthly payments. On existing loans, these are a known. On potential new loans, tables of loan payments appear in books like the REALTY BLUE BOOK, and many financial calculators and computer programs can figure payments.

Constants offer a short cut to computing cash-on-cash returns and I have developed several guidelines to express that relationship (illustrated in the examples below).

Assume: $100,000 Property
                      9% Cap Rate
                      50% Down Payment – 50% loan ($50,000)

The variable in these examples is the constant, which is dependent on the annual loan payment.

CHET'S CONSTANT GUIDELINE #1

If the Constant is greater than the Cap Rate, the Cash-on-Cash Return will be less than the Cap Rate.

EXAMPLE:

$100,000 property with 9% Cap Rate returns $9,000 annually ($100,000 x 9% = $9,000)

$50,000 Loan with an **11% constant** has $5,500 payments ($50,000 x 11% = $5,500)

Cash Flow = $3,500 ($9,000-$5,500)

Cash-on-Cash return = 7% ($3,500 cash flow / $50,000 investment)

11% (Constant) is greater than 9% (Cap Rate) = Cash-on-Cash return will be less than 9%

CHET'S CONSTANT GUIDELINE #2

If the Constant is equal to the Cap Rate, the Cash-on-Cash Return will be equal to the Cap Rate.

EXAMPLE:

$100,000 property with 9% Cap Rate returns $9,000 annually ($100,000 x 9% = $9,000)

$50,000 Loan with a **9% constant** has $4,500 payments ($50,000 x 9% = $4,500)

Cash Flow = $4,500 ($9,000-$4,500)

Cash-on-Cash return = 9% ($4,500 cash flow / $50,000 investment)

9% (Constant) is equal to 9% (Cap Rate) = Cash-on-Cash return will be equal to 9%

CHET'S CONSTANT GUIDELINE #3

If the Constant is less than the Cap Rate, the Cash-on-Cash Return will be greater than the Cap Rate.

EXAMPLE:

$100,000 property with 9% Cap Rate returns $9,000 annually ($100,000 x 9% = $9,000)

$50,000 Loan with a **7% constant** has $3,500 payments ($50,000 x 7% = $3,500)

Cash Flow = $5,500 ($9,000-$3,500)

Cash-on-Cash return = 11% ($5,500 cash flow / $50,000 investment)

7% (Constant) is less than 9% (Cap Rate) = Cash-on-Cash return will be less than 9%

The relationships between constants and cap rates will be explored in more depth in the chapter on leverage.

Chapter 6
Tax Shelter

"The sky is falling, the sky is falling." Every time the IRS or a tax court comes down with an adverse ruling affecting real estate, or Congress plugs a loophole, some people run around like Chicken Little screaming that their financial world is coming to an end. Unfortunately many investors and brokers have treated tax shelter as the primary reason for investing in real estate. In years past, real estate has been granted some outstanding and unique tax advantages. This has sometimes led investors to ignore the real economics of real estate ownership.

In the early 1980s, when the prime rate was near 20% and real estate's allowed depreciable life was a short 15 years, real estate yields made no sense, but real estate as a tax shelter did. Real estate syndicators and stockbrokerage houses placed billions of their investors' funds into tax shelter development deals—apartment buildings, office, and research and development ("R&D") buildings—often without a realistic concern for the true economics. Overbuilding caused failures, and many areas of the United States paid the price. As a result Houston, Dallas, Denver, San Diego, San Jose and many other Sunbelt and energy-driven-economy cities experienced severe economic impacts. Tax shelter alone is not a viable reason for acquiring investment real estate.

What are the tax advantages of real estate? The 1986 Tax Reform Act limited real estate's most publicized tax shelter, the use of excess book depreciation to offset ordinary income. There remain some outstanding tax benefits through book depreciation, as covered in this chapter. The other big advantage lies in the tax deferred exchange, discussed in a later chapter.

Before we proceed, it is important to know that the tax laws affecting real estate change almost annually. During my 40 plus years as a broker, depreciation life has been as short as 15 years and in excess of 40 years. Long-term capital gain and installment sale reporting have changed, and then changed again. Even the tax-deferred exchange has come under attack. I will make no attempt to keep this book updated as to the most recent whims of Congress. Instead we will cover how the tax fundamentals operate, and the reader should always consult with his or her accountant regarding the latest updates.

BOOK DEPRECIATION

Book depreciation ("depreciation") allows the owner of real property (real estate) or business property (business personal property) to deduct funds to replace obsolete or worn-out equipment and buildings from taxable income while, in fact, no money is being spent. Certain items, including machinery, computers and automobiles, actually do lose value through wear or obsolescence. But, most real estate is different. Instead of decreasing in value, historically, most real properties actually command a higher price each year.

Depreciation, a non-money expense, can make a property with positive cash flow into one that shows a tax loss. The extent of the loss depends on five factors:

1. THE IMPROVEMENT-LAND RATIO;
2 THE ECONOMIC LIFE OF THE IMPROVEMENTS;
3. SPECIAL TAX INCENTIVES IN EFFECT AT THE TIME;
4. Use of COMPONENT OR COMPOSITE DEPRECIATION; and
5. Election of STRIGHT-LINE OR ACCELERATED DEPRECIATION

FACTOR #1—THE IMPROVEMENT-LAND RATIO

For income tax purposes, business and income property owners are allowed to depreciate buildings but not land. Therefore, an equally priced property with a higher ratio of improvements to land has more depreciation expense than one with a lower improvement-land ratio. For example, let's compare two $200,000 properties. One $200,000 property is a four-unit apartment building, which consists of a $160,000 building constructed on a $40,000 lot. The second $200,000 property consists of a $100,000 commercial building constructed on a $100,000 lot. Provided both properties had the same economic life and both used the same depreciation method, we would be able to depreciate $160,000 of our $200,000 apartment investment (75%-25% improvement-land ratio), while we can only depreciate $100,000 of the commercial building investment (50%-50% improvement-land ratio). If both buildings had a 25 year life (not the current tax law) and both used straight-line reporting (an equal depreciation amount each year) the apartment building would provide the owner an annual depreciation expense loss of $6,400 ($160,000 divided by 25) while the commercial building would provide the owner with a loss of only $4,000 ($100,000 divided by 25).

How do we determine the improvement-land ratio? Rather than hiring an appraiser, most real estate investment brokers and knowledgeable investors let the county tax appraiser do the work. In order to determine property values for taxation purposes, the county tax assessor periodically appraises each property in the county and these values are broken down into land, improvements and personal property. The results of these appraisals are available for public inspection in the county tax assessor's office and in most title company offices.

The appraisal entry for a $200,000 four-unit apartment building might appear: L 30,000, I 112,500, P 7,500. The "L" stands for land value, "I" for improvements, and "P" for personal property.

According to the assessor, the property's total value is $150,000 (L+I+P). We can determine our improvement-land ratio by dividing the values into the total. Land is 20% of the total ($30,000/$150,000); improvements are 75% of the total ($112,500/$150,000); and personal property is 5% of the total ($7,500/$150,000).

Now that we have our ratios, we can apply them to our purchase price. Don't worry about the fact that the assessor values the property at $150,000 and you are paying $200,000. Tax appraisals are almost always different (and usually lower) than the purchase price and we are only using the tax assessor's ratios, not values.

Of our $200,000 price, 20% or $40,000 is assigned to land; 75% or $150,000 is assigned to improvements and 5% or $10,000 to personal property.

If you don't like the assessor's ratio and feel that you can justify a more advantageous improvement-land ratio, then use your better ratio, but be prepared to prove your case if challenged by the IRS.

FACTOR #2—ECONOMIC LIFE

Economic life, for income tax purposes, is the number of years the improvement (building or personal property) is expected to last before losing its economic viability. In reality, it is an artificial number set by the U. S. Congress to encourage or discourage investments. By designating a shorter economic life, the government promotes investment in that category of property. For example, if it became socially desirable (or garnered more votes) to build more low income housing units, Congress could give a shorter economic life to low rent apartments, regardless of their true economic life. As Congress seems to change its focus bi-annually, allowed economic life policies experience constant modifications. At the time you are reading this, all properties may have the same economic life or different buildings may have radically different lives.

All things being equal, the shorter the economic life, the faster an improvement can be written off and the greater the amount of depreciation that can be taken each year. For instance, a brand new concrete industrial building may have a 50-year economic life, while a 30-year old apartment house may only have 10-years remaining economic life. Presuming both improvements cost $200,000 and both use straight-line depreciation, the tilt-up concrete building would allow the investor to take only 2% annual depreciation ($200,000 / 50 years = $4,000 per year, or 2%). The old apartment building with its 10-year remaining life would allow the investor to depreciate 10% ($200,000 / 10 years= $20,000 per year, or 10%).

FACTOR #3—SPECIAL TAX INCENTIVES

Congress, from time to time, has special tax incentives dealing with economic life. Typical examples of these are the aforementioned shorter life (or faster write-off, if you prefer) or investment tax credits, for some low-income housing and historical properties. Check with your tax advisor to determine what incentives are available and what properties qualify under the current law.

FACTOR #4—COMPONENT OR COMPOSITE DEPRECIATION

At certain times, the investor can also choose to take component or composite depreciation. "Composite depreciation" is the depreciation of a building in its entirety over its useful economic life. The previous example of the comparative economic life of the industrial building and the apartment building used composite depreciation.

"Component depreciation" is the taking of separate depreciation based on the varied economic lives of all major parts of a building. For example, a building shell might have an economic life of 50 years, the air conditioner 15 years, the office carpets 7 years, the roof 20 years, and the plumbing and electrical 25 years.

FACTOR #5—STRAIGHT-LINE OR ACCELERATED DEPRECIATION
This is another government tax incentive system, and the type of depreciation method that can be taken will change with Congress and the economy. Basically, depreciation falls into two categories— Straight-line and Accelerated. Before deciding on depreciation methods the property owner should consult with his tax advisor on the recapture provisions of the current tax law.

STRAIGHT-LINE depreciation is taken when the investor elects to depreciate an equal amount each year, using all of the depreciation over the economic life of the improvement. Example: 25-year life, $200,000 improvement, straight-line depreciation would give the investor 4% per year ($8,000 each year) for 25 years. The proof: $8,000 X 25 years = $200,000. Your accountant can tell you when you need to consider salvage value, residual value at the end of the economic life.

ACCELERATED DEPRECIATION has taken several forms over the years, including 200% declining balance, 150% declining balance, 125% declining balance and sum-of-the-digits. Generally, the higher percentages (i.e. faster write-offs) have been given to residential income properties to promote housing and to new buildings to promote new construction.

Presuming the 150% declining balance option is currently available, the taxpayer would be permitted to take 150% of the straight-line depreciation rate. Using the straight-line example, 150% of 4% is 6% per year. However, the amount of the improvement expense is not static; it is a declining balance that is reduced in each successive year by the previous year's deduction.

In year one, the taxpayer can deduct an improvement expense of $12,000, or 6% of $200,000. However, in year two, the taxpayer must subtract $12,000 from the improvement expense before calculating the deduction ($200,000-$12,000=$188,000). Thus, the year two deduction is $11,280, or 6% of $188,000. In year three, the declining improvement expense of $176,720 ($188,000-$11,280) would result in a deduction of $10,603, 6% of $176,720. These calculations would continue throughout the economic life.

In times past, owners have been able to change from accelerated to straight-line depreciation. The investor should consult with tax counsel to determine what type of investment properties currently offer what types (if any) of accelerated depreciation.

OTHER INCENTIVES

Depending on the current tax laws, investment tax credits (ITC) on personal property may offer a large, one-time write-off for certain investment properties: hotels, motels, orchards and vineyards. The investor needs to check with a specialist in farm and ranch properties to make sure which year of growth the ITCs can be taken.

Chapter 7

Leverage

It has been said that given enough leverage, one man could move the world. I don't know about that, but I do know that given enough leverage a person could buy the world. However, when the first payment was due...

There is an old real estate joke about a promoter who rushed into his partner's office saying, "I've got good news and bad news. The good news is we can get the Empire State Building for $800,000,000. The bad news is they require a $10,000 deposit."

In physics, a lever can move a very heavy object using a much lighter object. In real estate, leverage is the common term for purchasing or controlling a larger property with little money.

The four big components of real estate investments are **property analysis**, playing the economic **cycles**, good **management** (covered later), and knowing when and how much to **leverage** investments. Many real estate "gurus" have preached leveraging all investments to the maximum. This advice works when inflation is driving prices up monthly, but it is very poor advice in up and down markets.

Leverage is the art of using other people's money to make money. Leverage, when combined with a keen eye for opportunities and a feel for the market, is the key to making big money in real estate. A $10,000 investment can buy a $10,000 property or a $100,000 property. By knowing the market, cap rates and growth areas and by spending the time to seek out good buys, the aggressive player can acquire properties that achieve 20% or more annual growth over a relatively short period. It may require leasing and/or fix-up efforts, but these returns are available. And, if the 20% return property is not locally available, the player must be willing to expand his geographical area.

Let's look at the earning potential available from a well-leveraged investment. A $100,000 property purchased for $10,000 with a 20% return is worth $140,000 after only two years, providing a profit of $40,000 or 400%. $50,000 in equity could be leveraged to acquire a $500,000 building that makes 40% (20% per year) over two years. The investor would then have $250,000 in equity to put into even larger properties.

The larger investor, starting with one million dollars, could be holding $20 million within a few years. And, as long as the protection afforded by IRS Section 1031 remains intact, all of this growth can be achieved without the estate being diluted by taxes taken at each step.

Buying a million dollar property with one hundred thousand dollars down payment would be considered a highly leveraged transaction. Buying with 25% down would be considered moderately leveraged and 50% down would be low or lightly leveraged.

INVESTOR LEVERAGE RATIOS
50% Loan-to-Value - Low leverage
75% Loan-to-Value - Moderate leverage
90% Loan-to-Value - High leverage

As discussed in an earlier chapter, real estate ownership has three primary benefits—yield, growth and tax shelter. Leverage has a major impact (either positive or negative) on each of these benefits. Understanding leverage and using it intelligently is the key to wealth in real estate. Conversely, ignoring the downside risk of taking highly leveraged ownership positions has destroyed many real estate fortunes. We will examine the impact of leverage in detail.

Leverage allows the investor to acquire much larger properties with the same funds. For example, the investor with $100,000 has the choice of acquiring a $100,000 property, a $300,000 property, a $500,000 property, or possibly even a $1,000,000 property. If the real estate purchased is appreciating, the $1,000,000 property could have ten times the appreciation as the $100,000 property. (If each property increases in value 5% per year, the $100,000 property increases in value $5,000 while the $1,000,000 property increases in value $50,000, a 50% return on the investment!)

This chapter contains formulas and graphs which will assist the numbers-oriented investor in understanding the principles of leverage. The reader less numbers-oriented should not make these formulas a stumbling block to your continuing reading the book. A mastery of these formulas is not necessary, but an understanding of the concept is vital to successfully invest in real estate.

A. THE IMPACT OF LEVERAGE ON YIELD
Again, leverage is the art of using other people's money to make money. Originally leverage was used to multiply yield. When I first entered investment real estate brokerage in 1965, buyers would expect properties to have a "yield" (cap rate) of 2% higher than the interest rate on the loan. They called this their "2% spread." This would allow the investor to make a profit on each borrowed dollar. If we can borrow money at 7% interest and invest it at 9% return, other things being equal, it is good business.

The SPREAD is a key to understanding impact of leverage on yield. The spread is the difference, positive or negative, between what the property earns and the interest paid to the lender(s). A spread is **positive** when the property cap rate is higher than the composite of interest rates on the loans. A spread is **negative** when that interest rate is higher than the cap rate.

POSITIVE SPREAD LEVERAGE

To illustrate the impact of leverage on yield, we will examine a positive spread situation. Assume we purchased a $100,000 property with a 9% cap rate, subject to a $75,000 loan, at 7% interest, with an 8% constant. The $75,000, 7% loan has first year's interest of $5,250, and the annual payments with an 8% constant total $6,000.

In leveraged investments the investor and the lender are BOTH investors in the property. In this example the investor invests $25,000 and the lender invests $75,000. The lender has invested three times as much the investor. This is a 3:1 lender-investor ratio.

The property is earning nine percent on the entire $100,000 ($9,000). The investor receives 9% on his $25,000 ($2,250), while the lender receives only 7% on his $75,000 investment, leaving the remaining 2% of $75,000 or $1,500 as additional profit to the investor.

Not all of the $1,500 is cash flow. One percent of $75,000 or $750 goes back to the lender for principal pay-down (portion of the payment that goes to principal reduction on the loan), while the other $750 goes to the investor as additional cash flow. The result is that the investor receives $2,250 plus $750, or $3,000 total cash flow.

On a $25,000 investment this would be a 12% cash-on-cash return, and a 15% total return to the investor.

There is a 15% total return because the investor received 2% on the lender's investment and the lender invested three times the amount the investor invested ($75,000 vs $25,000). From this we create a formula that covers all situations.

SPREAD FORMULA

Loan Amount multiplied by variable "x" plus NOI equals Profit;
Profit as a percentage of investment equals Total Return

If the borrower in the above example had been able to borrow $90,000,
his/her investment would have been $10,000, a lender-investor ratio of
9:1. Using a positive spread of 2% and an NOI of $9,000 ($100,000
property x 9% cap rate), the calculation to determine the total return
on investment would appear:
[$90,000 (Loan) * x] + $9,000 = $2,700 (Profit);
$2,700 (Profit) / $10,000 (Investment) = 27% (Total Return)
The spread is still 2%.

The Result:
($90,000 * 2%) + 9% = 27% $10,000

Using dollars, the example would look this way:
Property Value $100,000 Income = 9% = 9,000; $90,000 loan @ 7%
Interest = (6,300) Profit $2,700; As a return on a $10,000 Investment
27% = total return

Often properties do not have a 2% positive spread. In many cases, the
loan constant, and even interest rates, are HIGHER than cap rates. This
creates a negative spread. Our example will assume a 10% loan interest
rate and an 11% constant.

When we borrow at an interest rate higher than the property cap rate,
the cost of borrowing not only uses all of the return from the lender's
portion of the investment, but requires a portion of the investor's return,
as well, to cover the shortfall in the lender's portion. In addition, all loan
principal payments will have to come from what would have been the
owner's return.

The following example illustrates a negative spread.

NET OPERATING INCOME:	($100,000 Property * 9% cap rate)	= $9,000
Less: LOAN INTEREST:	($75,000 * 10%)	= $7,500
Equals: TOTAL RETURN		= $1,500

B. GROWTH LEVERAGE

Using the same $100,000 property, we will see how leverage affects our investment with 25% down and with 10% down.

Assume a growth market, in which properties are increasing in value at 5% per year, a $100,000 building would increase $5,000 per year. On a $25,000 investment this is a 20% annual return ($5,000 / $25,000).

The same building still returns $5,000 with $10,000 down, but now that $5,000 represents a 50% annual return on the $10,000 investment ($5,000 / $10,000).

The following chart, a growth multiplier, shows the profits on invested capital if the property value increases or decreases by 2%, 5% and 10%. The figures with minus signs are losses.

GROWTH MULTIPLIER

%	Positive Annual Growth				Negative growth—(recession)		
Down	+10	+5	+2	0	-2	-5	-10
	Annual Investment Appreciation				Annual Investment		Loss
10	100%	50%	20%	0	-20%	-50%	-100%
15	66.7%	33.3%	13.3%	0	-13.3%	-33.3%	-66.7%
20	50%	25%	10%	0	-10%	-25%	-50%
25	40$	20%	8%	0	-8%	-20%	-40%
30	33.3%	16.7%	6.7%	0	-.6.7%	-16.7%	-33.3%
33.33	30%	15%	6%	0	-6%	-15%	-30%
40	25%	12.5%	5%	0	-5%	-12.5%	-25%
50	20%	10%	4%	0	-4%	-10%	-20%

If the investor highly leverages the investment, buying with only 10% down, and the property value increases at 10% per year, the investor will create 100% annual growth profit on the investment. The chart points out what happens with various percentages of positive and negative growth and various down payments.

LEVERAGING GROWTH REAL ESTATE IS THE WAY TO BECOME REAL ESTATE RICH – OR REAL ESTATE POOR

LEVERAGE AND RISK

I once owned a free and clear office building that lost money, but it is generally pretty difficult to get in too much financial trouble owning unencumbered real estate. The risk is so negligible that it really takes an unusual set of circumstances to have negative cash flow without loans. However, as you may have noted on the growth multiplier chart, owning free and clear real estate is not necessarily the quickest way to wealth. Leveraging growth real estate is the winning way. But, it also has the highest risk— the greater the leverage, the higher the risk. So, if leverage is the name of the game, we need to be able to evaluate the risk.

On the growth multiplier chart we examined what happens to leveraged properties in a down market. The highly leveraged properties lose big. And, although I was a perennial optimist, markets do go down and the intelligent player needs to be prepared for that eventuality.

There are two potential dangers when using leverage. There is the short-term danger of losing income from rental properties and the second danger is having the property value decrease below the loan amount. Vacancies can quickly turn a positive cash flow property into an "eater", and rent strikes and nonpaying tenants are common culprits. Properties owned free and clear can handle vacancies and other problems, but those highly leveraged cannot—unless the owner is prepared to feed his budding "alligator."

One of the most commonly asked questions by novice investors is, "How highly can I leverage a property before the property begins to experience negative cash flow?" I have developed a very simple formula to answer this question. THE CAP RATE DIVIDED BY THE CONSTANT EQUALS THE BREAK-EVEN PERCENTAGE.

Using my formula, I can tell you that we can place no less than an $82,000 loan on a $100,000 building with an 11% constant and a 9% cap rate in order to have the property break even.
9% (Cap Rate) / 11% (Constant) = 82% (Loan-to-Value to Break Even)

LEVERAGE SUMMARY:
In **Boom** times, high leverage is an outstanding estate building tool. In **Bust** times, it can, and does, ruin property owners. During the Boom days of 2000-2006, many made millions borrowing to the maximum on every project. These same owners saw their assets totally disappear when property values cratered, and tenants vacated. Not only did their equity evaporate, but the bank, after foreclosing, came to collect on personal guarantees that were required of owners in order to originate the high leverage loans. Owners not only lost their entire investment, but ended up using all of their other assets to satisfy the banks' deficits. Often the result for the investor was bankruptcy.

So what is **Beyond** this most recent Boom and Bust? In 2010, the capital markets are constipated. Even if the borrower wanted to leverage his/her property, institutional loans are not available. And private lenders, while not as regulated, are more cautious, and are scraping for investor funds to lend.

In these chaotic times, I believe that the investment of choice, for the average investor, is well-located, free and clear real estate. Real estate is a commodity, but one with the added advantage of potential cash flow. If hyper-inflation hits, with the dollar continuing to lose worth, real estate will increase in value.

Instead of making an investor or seller a lender, make them a partner. A lender has a static fixed position with priority over the investor. A partner, while sharing in the upside, also shares in the downside, thus reducing all parties' risk. When the market rebounds, most of us will be very careful about using extreme leverage to build our estates.

Chapter 8
Managing Real Property

Good property management cannot save a bad property in poor economic times. But bad property management can destroy a potentially successful investment, anytime.

Good property management can create value, provide comfort to owners and make real estate ownership a pleasurable experience. Poor management can result in lost revenues, property devaluation, and time in court.

When I started my first brokerage business in San Jose, California in the 1960s, one of the first "divisions" I opened was a property management section. I generally ignored it, it never prospered and within a year I closed it down. Since then, I have personally owned and managed dozens of properties and have come to realize that there is nothing particularly mystical about managing real estate. Success requires common sense, attention to detail, good people skills, time management, a good accounting system, honest employees, knowledge of tenant/landlord law, and the ability to deal calmly with stressful situations.

All properties require some amount of management. Even bare land requires someone to pay the property taxes and attend zoning meetings if any adjacent properties are requesting rezoning. No one wants to wake up one morning to find that a tallow works has been given a building permit upwind of your luxury apartment site, or that your commercial corner has been rendered valueless because the community general plan has been changed to only allow a park in that location.

But, intense management comes with owning improved property. It encompasses tenant acquisition, screening and relations, property maintenance, supplies, outside contractor selection and coordination, rent collection and accounting. A well managed property will be maintained with no deferred maintenance and will be fully occupied with qualified, contented tenants paying market adjusted rents on time. The owner or owner's agent should be kept informed of any changes in status. Spending should be tightly controlled. In commercial offices or industrial properties, all leases should provide for cost-of-living increases or reachable percentages.

The small property owner has a decision to make. Should I manage the property myself or hire a property management firm? There is no right answer. It depends on the owner and the property. If you are handy, like to maintain your own property, enjoy interacting with people, and can be tough when necessary, then you may choose to manage your own properties. If, like me, you don't particularly like working around the house and are a sucker for a sad story, you are probably better off paying a property manager a standard fee of 5% to 10% of rental income to run the property.

ACQUIRING TENANTS

The specifics of acquiring a tenant or tenants will vary with the type of property. A single family home or a small apartment building will require a much simpler document than the lease on a 100,000 square foot commercial space. However, certain aspects are similar. In most cases some advertising is necessary, and in all cases some form of lease is mandatory.

Most small properties are rented either through a newspaper or internet ad or from a sign. Leasing on small properties is either done by the owners, property management firms, or on-site property managers. Large commercial and industrial properties are leased by commercial real estate leasing agents.

TENANT SCREENING

At one time or another every landlord has lamented: "I'm better off with no tenant than a bad tenant." Against better judgment, every long-term property owner has succumbed to a heart-wrenching story from a prospective tenant and subsequently rued the day they ever met the tenant. Besides not paying rent, a bad tenant can destroy the property, create legal problems and generally cause the property owner to wish they had invested in the stock market.

I once overheard a tenant advocate paralegal on a call with a client who was being evicted for non-payment of rent. It seemed that the tenant hadn't paid in three or four months and the landlord was finally about to get them out. The tenant wanted advice on how to prolong their free stay. The paralegal asked "Are there any bugs in the house?" Pause. Then, "Are you sure, not even any ants?" Then, "Well, there could be cockroaches, too, couldn't there?" While the conversation was going on I was internally dying for that poor unknown landlord. I envisioned some hard working couple busting their ass to get ahead, fighting to keep their mortgage current, and here was a free-loading tenant conspiring with a do-gooder paralegal to cheat the property owner out of even more rent, creating added legal costs, plus additional time and worry.

Drug dealers are a very real problem in residential rentals. Homes and apartments can be taken over by these undesirables, creating havoc in entire buildings and neighborhoods. The only answer is careful and thorough screening prior to renting the space. A credit report and references are a must. The owner or property manager must not only check with the present landlord (who might say anything just to be rid of a problem), but prior landlords as well. Appearances can deceive. Obviously we are all attracted to clean, healthy, well-dressed people, but the same screening standards should be applied to all applicants.

PROPERTY MANAGEMENT COMPANIES

Property management firms come in all sizes and specialties. Some only handle single family residences and maybe duplexes. Others manage apartment buildings. Others may specialize in commercial properties or by properties by industry, like shopping centers. Because so much of an investor's financial success depends on quality property management, due diligence should be performed before selecting a property management firm.

1) What are the fees?

2) What services are provided for these fees?

3) What else will I be charged for?

4) Do you mark-up materials, contractor's work, and supplies?

5) Who pays the on-site manager?

6) How often will I get income and expense statements (should be monthly), and what will they look like?

7) Are you bondable or bonded?

8) How is the money handled and accounted for?

And, finally, get references and check them out.

Although not always required by law, I recommend that owners have an on-site manager. Even if it is only a duplex, someone responsible is needed on-site. A $10 rent reduction can save the owner from being called out in the middle of the night to shut off an angle stop on a leaky faucet.

In larger properties, the management team may consist of an off-site or professional property management company supervising an on-site management team: leasing agent(s) (if none on staff), maintenance personnel, and independent contractors. The professional management company will handle all accounting, rent collection, bill payment, and report monthly on all of the above to the owner or owner's agent.

MAINTAINING THE PROPERTY

On paper, the owner, property management company or tenant may be responsible for maintaining the property. But, no matter what the contract says, the owner is ultimately responsible. And if the property management company is unsatisfactory, the owner must step in to replace them.

Theories on how best to maintain properties abound. Obviously, if you can get the tenant to be responsible they will not complain about the condition of the premises. Many knowledgeable investors provide tenants' rent reductions in exchange for maintaining and upgrading a property.

In theory, properties should be well maintained at all times. And properties throwing off adequate cash flow are generally well kept. Unfortunately, many marginal properties are unable to provide sufficient capital to cover all of the needed maintenance. This can lead to a downward spiral: poor maintenance equates to fewer tenants, even less income and even more deferred maintenance. The problem often starts with an unrealistic expectation of maintenance costs. It costs money to own rentals. Most proformas on small income properties either lie about real costs, or ignore them. Carpets wear out, paint fades, cracks and peals. Water pipes break. Tenants knock holes in walls and doors. Kids mark up walls. Roofs wear out and leak.

A realistic budget needs to be planned and funds set aside for both wear and tear and emergencies, which are bound to occur. If the funds aren't available, the owner had better be prepared to do the work himself/herself or bring in a partner with money.

MAINTAINING TENANTS

It costs money to change tenants, so it's good business to keep good tenants happy. Prompt, personal attention to maintenance requests not only builds tenant loyalty but can save money by preventing even more expensive repairs. In larger complexes, newsletters and group activities are commonly used to create a sense of community.

It is important to have a set of fair, easy to understand rules, and then enforce them. If no dogs are allowed, or if loud music is prohibited after 10 PM, these provisions must be in the lease, and if violated, enforced.

Rents should be raised and lowered to reflect market conditions. One successful apartment property manager told me that when the units they managed were 100% full with a waiting list, the rents were too low and needed to be raised. He felt that if he maintained around 95% occupancy he was near to the top of the market and the rents were about right. Less than 90% and he felt his rents were too high.

Often, there is reluctance to raise rents amongst owners of single family homes and small income properties. They may have built a rapport with their tenants, know their problems, and hate to be perceived as the bad guy who takes more money from those who might not be able to afford it.

It's a tough call, but understand that buyers of income property buy on existing rents. Mrs. Jones may have been a great tenant for the past seven years, but if she is paying $400 a month and her two bedroom unit should bring $600, the property has been devalued by one-third. There is some middle ground. Long-time, loyal tenants can be given a break. Perhaps a small rental increase every six months will allow Mrs. Jones the opportunity to adjust her expenses but still keep her rent within shouting distance of real market rents.

In times of high vacancy, there is enormous pressure to get commercial tenants. Rent concessions can run as high as two years free on a five year lease. Commercial brokers patrol the sidewalks of shopping centers and the halls of office buildings attempting to steal tenants for their clients' buildings. To defend against these tactics, the existing landlord may have to make painful business decisions. Should I drastically cut the rent to save the tenant? Can I afford to lose the tenant? Can I get another tenant? If so, will I have to make the same concessions needed to keep the existing tenant? There are no easy answers. If the owner can weather the storm, it may be better to keep the property full at two-thirds of the income than to let it go vacant.

Full-time professional commercial brokers and property managers can assist in these decisions. For self-managed properties, the owner-manager needs to keep fully informed on market conditions, market rents, and trends in the community, which affect the real estate investment.

Chapter 9
Exchanging

In its simplest form, a real estate exchange differs from a real estate sale in that an exchange involves at least two properties, two acquiring parties and two disposing parties, while a sale usually involves one buyer, one seller and one property. Exchanging is a completely different real estate philosophy. Exchange-oriented investment brokers are necessarily aware of many alternate marketing methods and are very often able to achieve a vastly superior result for a client because of this type of broker creativity.

Exchanging has been very good to me over the past three decades and I have been able to make some contributions to the real estate exchange community. I developed my exchange skills almost by accident. With a free morning early in my real estate career I decided to attend a meeting of the local San Jose, California exchange group. Not knowing what an exchange group did, I went to the meeting mostly out of curiosity. It didn't seem particularly stimulating, so I probably wouldn't have returned except that I was visited the following week by the group's director who asked me to become vice-president. After I accepted I decided that if I were to become involved I should learn something about exchanging, so I began to take courses. A local real estate school offered a course on the mechanics, and the California Association of Realtors had two very comprehensive week-long classes that led to the Certified Property Exchanger (now CCIM) designation. Rounding out my classroom education was Richard Reno's Profitable Real Estate Exchanging and Counseling and Marvin Starr's Exchanging Taxation seminar, taught over two weekends at the beautiful Carmel Valley Country Club. Concurrently, I was receiving my "experience" education by brokering small and then ever larger and more complicated exchanges.

Having now brokered some of the largest real estate exchange transactions in the country, I have formed strong opinions about exchanging. I believe the ability to put together a real estate exchange is one of the most valuable tools available to the broker and the investor. Brokers who are unable to structure a real estate exchange may cost a client thousands or millions of dollars.

TWO REASONS TO EXCHANGE:

An exchange is used instead of a sale for one of two distinct and separate reasons: to DEFER TAXES or to INCREASE MARKETABILITY. The distinction must be effectively understood by the broker, if the broker is going to be a successful exchangor. Marketing PROBLEM PROPERTIES requires a completely different strategy and environment than marketing salable properties for a TAX EXCHANGE. We will cover both types in this chapter beginning with the tax exchange.

THE TAX EXCHANGE

Most TAX EXCHANGES (also called tax deferred exchanges) involve salable properties, and the only reason to exchange a salable property is to defer taxes. Under Section 1031 of the Internal Revenue Code, the investor can exchange his/her investment property for another investment property of equal or greater value and defer the tax on the gain. Section 1031 is one of the reasons real estate is a great investment because it allows the investor to keep equity intact while estate building. The TAX

EXCHANGE contract differs from a sales contract, but the marketing program is the same as if the owner intended to sell the property.

Many top real estate tax attorneys have built their careers on Internal Revenue Code Section 1031. The language is surprisingly brief, and its interpretation controversial. Currently, there are at least 20 very important court cases interpreting Section 1031.

Exchanging is somewhat like working through a maze. It would not be nearly as much fun if the player only had to draw a line from point "A" to point "B" with no obstacles in the way. Section 1031, with the IRS and the court rulings regarding the Section, provides the obstacles—the turns in the maze—that we must successfully navigate to reach our goal. During the estate-building period, the goal for the serious player is to make maximum use of equity, losing none of it to the government in taxes.

Section 1031 provides that, with certain exceptions, no gain or loss is recognized where property that has been held by the taxpayer for productive use in a trade or business, or for investment, is exchanged solely for property of a "like kind", to be held either for productive use in a trade or business, or for investment.

To clarify: "like kind" means (1) real estate for real estate, and (2) the real estate must be property held for investment or for use in trade or business. It is probably easier to explain what "like kind" is not than what it is. So, it's okay to exchange a farm for an apartment or a commercial building for bare land as long as they are both held for investment purposes. But, the investor cannot exchange investment properties for non-investment properties. For example, the investor cannot exchange his personal residence for investment properties. (The residence for residence exchange is covered separately under Section 1034 of the Code.)

Other non-investment properties that don't qualify under Section 1031 are "dealer" properties. Dealer properties are those held as inventory for sale, such as lots or houses subdivided by a developer.

Another exchange that does not qualify as tax deferred is real property for personal property. What is personal property? Anything that is not real property is personal property, including cash, mortgages, boats, airplanes, stocks, and partnership interests. Anything coming out of an exchange that is not "like-kind" is called "boot" and is taxable, with a couple of exceptions.

The bottom line is that investment real properties can be exchanged for investment real properties, tax deferred, as long as the owner receives no net cash, no net mortgage relief (NMR), a reduction of loan amounts owed because of the exchange, or other unlike property from the transaction. In order not to receive unlike property ("boot"), the property being acquired must be of equal or greater value than the property being exchanged, both in equity and total value. If the property owner does not exchange for another property of equal or greater value, then something of value must be received in the exchange to balance equities, and that something is boot and is taxable. An exchange can be completely tax deferred, partially or entirely taxable, depending on the unlike property taken out.

To fully understand the impact of exchanging, we need to have some knowledge of capital gains computations and the tax laws affecting sales of real estate investment properties. In addition, we need to understand some real estate tax terms.

No attempt should be made to close a transaction that could involve severe tax liability without the assistance of a qualified tax advisor conversant with Section 1031.

ADJUSTED TAX BASIS (BOOK VALUE)
The amount of potential tax liability in a real estate sale or exchange depends on the amount of gain the seller receives. In order to compute potential gain we must first compute the ADJUSTED TAX BASIS ("basis") or BOOK VALUE. The "basis" on a property purchased is computed as follows:

PURCHASE PRICE
+ ACQUISITION CLOSING COSTS
(-) ACCUMULATED DEPRECIATION
+ CAPITAL IMPROVEMENTS
+ SELLING COSTS
= ADJUSTED TAX BASIS

Example:

Purchase Price	$450,000
+ Acquisition closing costs	5,000
(-) Accumulated depreciation	(100,000)
+ Capital Improvements (i.e. swim pool)	15,000
+ Selling costs	30,000
= Adjusted Tax Basis	$400,000

GAIN

The amount subject to tax on the sale of real estate is the GAIN. Gain is computed by subtracting the adjusted tax basis (or book value) from the sales price.

Example:

Sales Price	$600,000
(-) Adjusted tax basis	(400,000)
= Gain	$200,000

The seller pays tax (either short or long term capital gains, if capital gains are in vogue) on the $200,000. By exchanging properties the seller is able to partially or completely defer this gain.

INDICATED GAIN and RECOGNIZED GAIN

To better understand what is taxable and what can be deferred, the real estate investment brokerage community has coined these two additional terms.

INDICATED GAIN is the taxable gain explained above that a seller would pay if a sale occurs.

RECOGNIZED GAIN is the portion of the indicated gain that is actually taxable, or, in other words, the portion that is not deferrable. In a sale, indicated and recognized gains are the same. However, in an exchange, recognized (or taxable) gain is the total unlike property received, the combination of CASH RECEIVED, NET MORTGAGE RELIEF, and OTHER BOOT, or the INDICATED GAIN, whichever is smaller.

EXAMPLE OF A SECTION 1031 EXCHANGE:
Mr. Jones owns a $300,000 six-unit apartment building with a $155,000 loan and he wishes to exchange his equity into a $600,000 twelve-unit apartment building owned by Ms. Smith, who has a $340,000 loan. Smith has a $400,000 adjusted tax basis.

Structure:
When attempting to structure an exchange, it is important to remember that what we are doing is exchanging equities. This structure is the "T" approach, and the one used by most exchangers.
(I don't know why it's called a "T", but it is.)

JONES		SMITH
6-Unit		12-Unit
$300,000	Price	$600,000
155,000	(-) Loans	340,000
145,000	(=) Equity	260,000

The difference in equities is $115,000. In order to balance equities, the party with less equity must make up the difference. One of the following could be used:

1) Jones to give Smith $115,000 in cash; or
2) Jones to execute a $115,000 note to Smith, secured by a second mortgage against the 12-unit; or

3) Jones to refinance the 12-unit for $455,000, the $115,000 net loan proceeds to Smith; or

4) Jones to give Smith $115,000 in other personal or real property equities.

The balancing of the equities can also be a combination of the above. For purposes of our example, let's assume Jones gives Smith $65,000 cash and a $50,000 note to balance.

Tax Consequences:
Looking at Jones first, if he receives cash, net mortgage relief, or other boot, he will be taxed to the extent that cash given does not offset the cash received, NMR or other boot.

Does Jones receive any cash? No. Jones gives Smith $65,000 cash.

Does Jones receive net mortgage relief? No. Jones increases his mortgage indebtedness from $155,000 to $340,000—an increase of $185,000.

Does Jones receive other boot? Not a bit.

So the transaction is totally tax deferred for Jones.

What about Smith?
Cash? Yes, $65,000.

Net mortgage relief? Yes. Smith gets relieved of a $340,000 mortgage and only takes on a $155,000 loan so she has net mortgage relief of $185,000.

What about other boot? Yes. Smith receives a $50,000 note from Jones. A note is personal property, therefore, "unlike" property.

Jones		Smith
0	Cash	$ 65,000
0	(+) Net Mortgage Relief	185,000
0	(+) Boot	50,000
0	(=) Total Unlike Property	$300,000

Smith receives unlike property valued at $300,000. However, Smith cannot pay more than her indicated gain. As her basis in the building is $400,000 and the transfer price is $600,000, her indicated gain is only the difference of $200,000. So, Smith's tax liability is $200,000. Naturally, Smith isn't making this exchange for tax reasons, unless she has some large usable tax losses elsewhere. Her incentive would be a marketing incentive.

THE DELAYED EXCHANGE

Until the 1970s all properties in an exchange needed to close concurrently in order for the exchange to qualify as tax deferred. This proved to be a roadblock that caused severe hardships on occasion, and ultimately court cases and IRS rulings allowed for a delayed, or "Starker," exchange. There are some very strict rules covering the closing of tax-deferred exchanges. The handling of money on all exchanges and the timing if the delayed exchange format is chosen must be followed carefully or an exchange can be successfully challenged by the IRS.

The present tax rules covering a delayed exchange provide 45 days from the date of closing a relinquished property for the exchangor to identify up to three replacement properties, and 180 days from the date of closing a relinquished property to close on one or more of the identified replacement properties. There are several other rules, but all delayed exchanges must use the 45/180 day schedule.

Professional accommodators are available to hold the funds and they become a party to the exchange. It is important to have a reliable accommodator as they have control of the sales proceeds from the relinquished property. Most major title insurance companies now offer accommodator services, and there are some very well qualified independent accommodator firms. Rates vary. The exchangor needs to carefully check out the firm's qualifications and rates.

Example of an award-winning Tax Exchange:

FROM SEA TO SHINING SEA

The transaction started with a phone call in late December from my clients saying, "Let's exchange the fourplexes," and ended April 21st with the recording of 64 properties valued at over $13,000,000. Among the hundreds of people involved were 35 principals, 13 brokers and 14 lenders.

My clients had owned 47 fourplexes for 13 years. They were tired of the day-to-day management and wanted more passive investments. But, equally important, they needed to free up $1,100,000 quickly. They liked commercial properties and wanted an exchange transaction that would give them cash and less management intensive properties.

The decision was made to market the fourplexes individually to obtain the highest possible prices. In early January, I had 200 offering brochures printed, whereupon my clients decided for personal reasons to raise their collective price from $4,150,000 to $4,552,000, necessitating a reprint of the material. As real estate prices were increasing daily, I was not sure how adversely this price increase would affect the salability of the fourplexes.

During the reprinting, I attended a national marketing meeting to search for leased commercial or industrial properties valued between $4,552,000 and $8,000,000. I received several preliminary offers, subject to my being able to sell the fourplexes for all cash prior to escrow closing. My clients were interested in three of the properties offered: a downtown Denver office building, a Florida shopping center and a Hawaiian shopping center.

Within two weeks, the clients and I were on a plane, and over two days and 7,000 miles, we inspected properties from coast to coast. We made offers on shopping centers in Florida, Arizona and Idaho, each from the same developer-owner.

After much negotiation, we agreed to acquire the three centers with a 10% absolutely net return with the developer leasing back the vacancies for sufficient income to net my clients the 10%. In the meantime, all 47 fourplexes sold in nine days, at full price and for all cash to seller. Some involved exchanges, with the exchanged-in properties cashing out, so fourteen additional properties became involved.

The exchange:

DEVELOPER		CLIENTS	
Florida Center	$4,350,000	47 Fourplexes	$4,552,000
Arizona Center	2,377,710	Less costs (est.)	300,000
Idaho Center	840,000		
Value	7,567,710		4,252,000
Less loans:	Florida 3,150,000	Fourplexes	1,052,000
Arizona	-0		
Idaho	694,000		
Equity	$3,723,710		$3,200,000

In a separate escrow, concurrent but immediately following the exchange escrow, my clients placed a new $1,664,000 loan on the free and clear Arizona center. From this loan, $523,710 was paid to the developer to balance the equities, with the remaining $1,140,290 going to the clients. In 61 other escrows, the 47 fourplexes and 14 exchanged-in properties were cashed out by the developer.

Even though the buyers of the 47 fourplexes were convinced of the value, the lenders were not, and we were turned down by many banks and savings and loans. Eventually we found eight lenders willing to take some of the units. Unfortunately, by the time we located these lenders and they had completed their loan processing, our contract time limit of April 5th had expired. We were, however, able to obtain a closing extension from the shopping center owner to April 21st.

The developer and his attorney flew out on April 12th to sign closing papers, only to find that 13 fourplex loans had not been approved. We explored closing part of the exchange, but closing either the Florida or Arizona centers without the other would have caused my clients adverse tax consequences. The developer came up with the idea that we close the acquisition of all three centers with the brokers buying the $918,000 equity in the 13 fourplexes (subject to the existing sales contracts) with $178,000 down and developer carrying back a $740,000 second, all due in 55 days. This would give us time to obtain our loans.

To have sufficient funds, my clients agreed to allow the developer to leave $740,000 of an existing $840,000 second on the Florida center, to be paid from the proceeds of the 13 fourplexes second.

In order to close by April 21st, additional title and escrow staff were called in to work nights and weekends assisting the escrow officer who had already devoted the previous five weeks, full-time, to this escrow. At 9 p.m. on the 20th, we still were not sure we had all of the documents, but the county manager of the title company stuck his neck out and said "GO!" At 11 a.m. Eastern, 9 a.m. Mountain, and 8 a.m. Pacific on the 21st, documents were recorded concurrently transferring the 64 properties.

As a result of this deal, my clients increased their annual cash flow by approximately $140,000 and paid off a $1,100,000 judgment. The developer received all cash for his centers, and 33 other principals acquired investment properties

The California Association of Realtors awarded this exchange as the year's Most Outstanding Investment Transaction.

THE PROBLEM PROPERTY EXCHANGE

The second reason for exchanging is to increase the marketability of real estate. Some of us who focus on creative real estate transactions feel that this is the primary reason for exchanging. Much real estate is not readily salable. In fact, in 2010 we believe that most real estate is unsalable.

In Bust times, there are many more un-salable properties than salable ones. Many properties are unsalable at the price the owner demands; and some properties, regardless of price, are considerably more salable than others.

Bare desert or mountain land, unfit for planting, recreation or development, is the least salable property. Other potentially unsalable properties include vacant office buildings, older motels and single use buildings with leases expiring soon. Changes in the economy, the cost of money, the yield on alternative investments, and tax laws can sometimes change salable properties into un-salable ones. Homes (investment or personal residences) are typically the most salable of all properties because there are more users for them, but in 2010 many owners have loans that are greater than the property is worth.

The word unsalable does not roll off of my tongue easily, nor does it truly express the type of properties we deal with in exchanges. A better term is PROBLEM PROPERTIES. For the exchange broker, one challenge with the term "problem properties" is that most owners will not admit their properties are problem properties. In exchanging, we foster the attitude that one owner's PROBLEM is another owner's OPPORTUNITY.

For purposes of clarification, I have coined two definitions. 1) A PROBLEM PROPERTY is any property that is not a salable property. 2) A SALABLE PROPERTY is any property that can be sold under terms acceptable to the seller within a predetermined length of time established between the broker and the seller (typically 90 days is considered reasonable).

If, going in, the owner and broker are convinced they have a salable property at an agreed upon price and an acceptable marketing time is 90 days, then on the 91st day the property becomes a problem property.

We should not be judgmental about problem properties. Are they bad? No, they just are not salable. The problem can be any one thing, or a combination of things. Some of the problems encountered are: vacancy problems; negative cash flow problems; over-financing, under-financing, or poor financing; location; access; title problems; litigation; poor leases; functional obsolescence; or disrepair. However, the two biggest problems that affect the marketability of real estate are the price and the lack of flexibility by the owner.

Within reason, almost all real estate can be marketed AT SOME PRICE. For various reasons, many owners are unwilling to keep reducing the price until they find a "thief," the buyer that may have no use for the property but will buy anything if it is cheap enough. Some owners CAN'T sell below a certain figure because of the loans on the property. But, more often, owners WON'T sell below a certain price. There is a lot of ego involved in taking a loss, or selling below what a neighbor received. So there is a bottom price the owners will place on most real estate, and thus many owners cause their salable properties to become problem properties by not meeting the real market where it is.

"What does this have to do with exchanging?" you ask. Well, working with experienced exchange brokers, the problem property owners can market their properties, usually not for cash, but for something they enjoy more than their present "problem property."

Problem properties require a non-traditional form of marketing. They are not effectively advertised though real estate ads in the newspapers or by placing a sign on the property. Instead they are promoted through exchange meetings, marketing forums where exchangors meet to brainstorm and market problem properties. Many of the most creative people in the real estate industry are the real estate exchangors. The top exchangors from around the country attend several exchange meetings a month, where we market our clients' and our own properties. We brainstorm the particularly difficult or timely problems. In a room holding 50 to 125 brilliant real estate professionals, ideas will be expressed; many will piggyback on the previous speaker's thoughts. Old "formulas" are brought out and new ones dreamed up. It is electrifying. This is synergism at its best.

The result is that problems get solved. An unmarketable property is marketed. My friend and top real estate exchanger, Bob Steele, catalogued the formulas that we use to market properties in creative real estate and, at last count, there were over 119 different marketing formulas, one of which is selling the property for cash.

How do we solve the problems and thus reduce the downside risk of making a bad real estate investment? The key to successful real estate exchanging is to have a very close client-broker relationship. Successful practitioners do extensive counseling with a client-candidate prior to agreeing to work on the client's problem property. Listing a salable property, by the very definition, gives the broker a high probability of selling success. This is not the case when dealing with a problem property. Without the full cooperation of a motivated and flexible client, attempting to market a problem property is a waste of everyone's time and money. I have established a set of criteria that potential clients must meet before I will work to solve their real estate problem:

THE PROBLEM PROPERTY LISTING TEST
1. The potential client and I have to agree that the property is a problem property. If the client feels that the property is salable, even though it has been listed with the twelve best brokers in the community for four years, we will never be able to market the property.
2. The client and I have to agree on what the problem is. Owners find it easy to tell the broker that they have run out of depreciation, or that they are tired of management, but it is very difficult to admit they made a bad buy in the first place or that they mismanaged it.
3. I must feel comfortable that the client is motivated to act. Often owners are merely interested in what might be offered for their property or what better investments might be out there. They are not serious about marketing their property. Richard Reno, the founder of modern

problem property exchanging, invented the term, "don't wanter." A "don't wanter" is a person who is truly motivated to change their real estate position, and not just for tax purposes. Maybe it's the two o'clock in the morning telephone call about the leaking pipe in the tenant's apartment, or the $125 monthly payment due on the land just after the owner has been laid off. There are many reasons why owners become don't wanters and I have heard most of them. Sometimes real estate ownership is like boat ownership: the two happiest days in a boat owner's life are the day he/she buys it and the day he/she sells it.

4. I must feel that I am competent to handle the problem. Sometimes I am not, or, more often, I may not be competent to handle all phases of the problem. If this is the case I will either not work on the problem, or I will put together a team with the ability to handle all phases of the problem.

5. I must feel that, considering the property and owner involved, there is a solution, and one with good odds of closing. Unfortunately, many who own problem properties live in hope that the real estate fairy will perform magic and come to the rescue. Others hope that a million to one offer will come in—the leased 7-11 market owner will love our little Nevada desert retreat and insist on taking the $800 per month payment off our hands. Maybe that happened somewhere, once, but we would all die broke if we depended on those kinds of miracles.

6. The client's third party influencers and I have to agree on a course of action. If I can't get cooperation from the client's attorney and CPA, the client needs to find another broker.

Most problem property owners do not pass the test, and I will not get involved.

If we play the real estate game long enough, none of us is so smart and so lucky that we won't have a problem property. We need to be rescued and the problem property exchange is our fire escape. An exchange can be the difference between taking a small loss (or no loss) and suffering a severe economic setback.

Abstract of an award-winning Market Driven Exchange

THE TRIANGLE

The cowboy stood 6' 7" in his stocking feet. I had never seen him in his stocking feet. I had never seen him in anything but well used cowboy boots, faded blue jeans and a cowboy shirt, rolled up at the wrist. He and his lovely wife had come to Puerto Vallarta, Mexico, to take the seminar I was teaching on Developing and Syndication. At least that was their excuse. They had really come to engage me to assist them in acquiring tax shelters and help them with their estate building program.

The cowboy's "aw shucks" demeanor and "good ole boy" facade hid a brilliant business mind and a wealth of real estate experience. A graduate of the University of California at Berkeley, he had started with Coldwell-Banker (back when there was a Coldwell and a Banker), and had developed and syndicated, as well as brokered, tens of millions of dollars in properties. He did not need me to teach him about real estate; but, like many truly successful people, he knew he did not know it all and that if he could get one good idea from me, the trip was worthwhile. Besides, Puerto Vallarta is lovely in January.

The cowboy and his business partner, a lawyer, had been very successful in buying large parcels of land in the path of progress, bringing in investors to replace their up-front money, and then selling the land to developers, carrying back loans secured by mortgages or trust deeds against the properties ("paper"). They had been so successful that they now had $13 million in paper, all paying 10% interest, which was all taxable as ordinary income. And the properties they were still holding were appreciating rapidly, so their tax problem was going to become even more acute.

Over lunch at a tropical oceanfront restaurant, the cowboy proposed that I represent him and his partner in acquiring tax shelters. Their problem was lack of cash. Like many that play the real estate game intensely, all available cash has already been invested or is needed for living expenses. But they did have the paper: notes, trust deeds and mortgages receivables.

Some months earlier, I had received a call from Bill Macbeth, a Yuma, Arizona broker and fellow member of the Society of Exchange Counselors who is also a CCIM (Certified Commercial Investment Member), the top designation in the field awarded by the National Association of Realtor's National Marketing Institute. Bill wanted me to jointly list a regional shopping center. Bill was very capable of brokering that center without my help, but he indicated he would be more comfortable if I was involved and that it would be fun to work together. I agreed to joint list the center provided I could get along with the owner and that the owner was flexible enough and/or the property was priced competitively enough that we would have a very real chance to market it.

We met with the owner, a CPA general partner of a group of three, who represented that he had full partnership authority in the marketing of the center. Although not overly friendly, the CPA seemed extremely motivated, so we entered into a listing contract. The listing price was $9,000,000 and the property had a $6,100,000 loan, leaving equity of $2,900,000. Based on income, the center was overpriced at the $9 million listing price; based on replacement cost, it was a bargain at that price.

After the meeting in Puerto Vallarta, I presented the center to the cowboy. He liked it and agreed to the $9 million price provided he could acquire it for $1 million in cash (which would be coming from a note pay-off) and $1.9 million of his paper, and he could assume the $6.1 million loan.

After a great deal of negotiation, the offer was accepted and an escrow opened. All of the inspections were made, the leases and mortgages reviewed, and then the closing date came—and went. The expected cash from the cowboy's note pay-off did not arrive. After two postponements, the transaction was cancelled.

At the same time, I was in the embryo stages of developing a new client, a multibillion dollar Savings and Loan (S&L) association. The chairman wanted to move non-earning assets into earning assets. We had presented several unaccepted offers to the S&L when the idea came to place the S&L in the middle of the cowboy/CPA transaction. The plan was to have the S&L exchange their houses and condos, owned through foreclosure, plus an equal amount of cash, for the cowboy's notes and trust deeds. To make the transaction more appealing for all parties, we added a 120-unit apartment building owned by the CPA to the transaction for an additional $3,800,000. We now had a three-way exchange involving $12,850,000 of the CPA's properties, the cowboy's paper and the S&L's free and clear houses, condos and cash.

Our original proposal was to have the S&L purchase the CPA's property equities for $4,094,449 and assume the existing loans, using one-half cash and one-half free and clear properties for the purchase. Then the S&L would sell the shopping center and the apartment equities to the cowboy for $4,094,449 in paper. The S&L's auditors did not like the structure of the transaction and they had us restructure it to have the cowboy purchase the CPA's properties with paper and then have the CPA exchange the paper to the S&L for half cash and half properties.

We spent fourteen months attempting to market the CPA's properties; eleven of the fourteen were after the cowboy had agreed to purchase and four followed the S&L's inclusion in the transaction. The closing involved 24 properties and totaled $14,900,000 in value.

The CPA group received their asking price and for their equity received $2,044,449 in cash and $2,044,449 in free and clear houses and condos. The cowboy was able to shelter nearly $900,000 with no cash outlay. The S&L moved $2,050,000 from non-earning to earning assets. They booked a profit, reduced their management, and moved $2,044,449 worth of properties out of their undesirable scheduled items category. Everybody won.

The National Association of Realtors awarded this transaction the Campbell Trophy for the best Commercial-Investment transaction in the United States in 1983.

Chapter 10
Estate Building

The successful investment estate building program is one that is approached methodically and with planning. I have designed a step-by-step approach to estate building that I have used with clients and teach to real estate investment brokers. The steps are:

1. Setting goals
2. Determining capabilities, flexibility and involvement
3. Determining comfort zones
4. Creating the plan
5. Acquiring the first property
6. Managing the asset
7. Pyramiding
8. Reaching the goals
9. Preserving the estate

Following these steps will afford the investor a sound basis for success in good and bad times.

1. SETTING GOALS

The hours spent setting goals may be the most important in estate building. Goal setting is not to be taken lightly. Beyond the physical attainment of a specific dollar amount or property acquisition, such non-material considerations as self-image are involved.

If we habitually set "unattainable" goals, or do nothing or little to achieve those goals, we will begin to think of ourselves as failures, unworthy or unlucky. Conversely, if we constantly set goals so low that achieving them brings no thrill or so easy that they require no stretch of imagination or skill, we will find life boring and experience no growth.

Setting estate building goals is a perfect time for us to take an in-depth look at our lives and where we are going. If we take the position that we can achieve anything we can conceive, provided we want it badly enough, then we go about the goal setting process a bit differently— knowing we are going to achieve our goals will make us more selective about what goals we choose. Perhaps making money is not as important as it seems, when the trade-off for money is time away from our family. On the other hand, maybe that trade-off isn't necessary. Maybe the trade-off is being better organized so there is more time for both making money and family.

What kind of goals should we be setting? The goals should be in writing, definitive, and with a time schedule for accomplishment. We need short- and long-term goals. The following might be a typical set of goals:

1. I will own my first real estate investment within 90 days of this date.
2. Within three years I will own properties with a total market value of no less than $500,000 and a true equity of no less than $150,000.
3. Within six years my real estate portfolio will be worth $1,300,000 and my equity no less than $450,000.
4. In year ten I will be able to pull $250,000 out of my $800,000 in real estate equities to start my twins at Yale. At that time, I will own $2,000,000 in real estate.
5. In year 20 I will own $7,000,000 in good cash flow properties and have $20,000 per month cash flow, most of it sheltered, making me independent of the need to work for money.

Each of us would go into more detail about what we expect our investments to do for us, our probable future monetary needs and the amount of time and energy we want to put into our estate building program. This brings us to our next step, which really needs to be integrated with the goal setting step: determining our capability, flexibility and involvement.

2. DETERMINING CAPABILITY, FLEXIBILITY & INVOLVEMENT

The more capable we are, the higher we can realistically set our goals. If we know nothing about real estate investments and "for damn sure don't intend to learn," we will be at the mercy of real estate brokers, developers, buyers and sellers who know more than we do. We won't know a good buy if it kicks us in the teeth. And worse, we won't know a bad one. The seller won't tell you, "My property is really a bad deal." None of us are born with real estate capabilities. They are learned over time and many of the lessons are costly.

This book is a primer. If you take the time to learn all that is written here, you will be more capable than 95% of real estate investors. But the winning player won't stop here. The winning players are perpetual students. They continue to read books and trade publications and constantly study the economic trends. They know growth areas and sluggish areas. They take potentially helpful seminars. The caliber of investors, developers, attorneys and brokers that take my "Developing, Syndicating and Big Money Brokerage" seminar are head and shoulders above their peers in their fields. They are winners and students.

We also must look at our financial capabilities. This will determine our financial starting point in the real estate game. The player coming out of the stock market with a million in cash will start at an entirely different level than the college student with great enthusiasm, but little money.

Financial capability encompasses more than the funds available for a down payment on a transaction. It includes how much we can add on a monthly basis—or how much we must take out of the property to support ourselves. Also, we must look at our ability to recover if we take a big loss trying for the big gain. The executive with a $250,000 per year salary would be able to take a completely different risk than a widow on social security.

Lay it all out in writing. How much can we invest in dollars? What will the property have to do for us in cash flow, or how much can we do for it in terms of putting money into the project? How much of our investment can we afford to lose? How capable are we of understanding and managing our investment? How much time are we willing to spend in the acquisition and management processes?

None of us will ever know everything there is to know about all of the possible real estate investments, but there are experts to help us. There are farm and land brokers, commercial brokers, industrial brokers and those that handle nothing but mobile home parks. There are hotel, motel and lodge specialists. Recreational land and time-share advisors are out there. And, competent, professional management is available in all of those areas.

Now let's evaluate our flexibility. The more flexible we are, the higher we can realistically set our goals. Every restriction we place on ourselves is one opportunity we exclude. For instance, if we say that we are never going to invest in a mobile home park because we all know mobile home parks are bad news, we have limited our flexibility and may pass up the best possible investment for us at that time. If we say that we won't even consider the convalescent hospital in Peoria, Illinois, because we refuse to own a property more than 50 miles from our house, we may inhibit our ability to reach our goals to such an extent that we must either realistically cut our goals in half or double our time schedule. I am not advocating that we should always be willing to go out of area or take every type of property offered, but we had better honestly evaluate the reason we are unwilling to make a particular move. Beyond a certain size it makes sense to consider geographical moves. When the estate builder moves into properties which are large enough to have competent professional management, then the location may make little difference, providing the location is a growth area and the economy stable.

Some best-selling real estate books preach that the way to make a million in real estate is to acquire structurally sound, cosmetically rundown apartment buildings and purchase them with little or no down payment. In a growth market, this is a superb formula. The problem is that if all of the estate builders are chasing after the country's structurally sound, cosmetically run-down apartment buildings, we will put such a demand on that limited inventory those fixers will become more valuable than new, clean apartment buildings. Are we a one-trick pony, or will we look at other opportunities?

But, we need to be honest about flexibility. If we are unwilling to acquire properties in high crime areas or move all over the country, acknowledge it. These decisions are not inherently right or wrong –they are right for us, and must be communicated to our broker.

The more involved we are willing to be; the higher we can realistically set our goals. The passive player will move much slower than the active investor. Activity can take many forms. It doesn't necessarily mean that we need to be out with a paint brush and a lawn mower, but that may help. It doesn't mean that we need to be able to replace a hot water heater or change a washer, but that can help, too. It can mean that the player is reading the real estate for sale column in the paper every morning, checking listings on Loopnet, and building a competent and energetic team of broker, attorney, accountant, and property managers. It may mean that the player is ready to jump on a plane to inspect a property with only a few hours notice and immediately make an offer with contingencies. It may mean that the player pays enough attention to the investments to notice when a manager is incompetent or dishonest. It may mean that the player is willing to take on a development project, a conversion, or renovate an old or run-down building.

Be realistic about your involvement. No games. Don't delude yourself. Are you really willing to spend the time that your specific goals will require? Where will that time come from? From your other work? From your family? From your golf, bowling or Monday night football?

3. DETERMINING COMFORT ZONES

What are our comfort zones with regard to debt and risk? Are we willing to put all of our life savings on one deal? Remember, the higher the risk, the higher the potential return. The more we are willing to leverage, the faster we might expect to reach our goals—but the greater the leverage, the greater is the risk that we will lose our entire investment.

When setting goals, it is important to define our comfort zones, recognizing that they will change as we become more experienced and confident. The beginning player may not wish to tackle a loan of more than 75% of the property value, while the more experienced player may seek to buy properties with 10% or no down payment. Over the years I have noted that the same clients who originally feared taking on a $100,000 mortgage now think nothing of assuming a $5 million dollar loan. And some have learned to regret it.

Maslow, the noted psychologist, in his "hierarchy of needs" tells us that we are all motivated to fulfill certain needs, from the most basic physiological ones of food, drink, shelter and the avoidance of pain, to safety and security. When those are satisfied, the needs for belonging, esteem and, ultimately, self-actualization need to be satisfied. Because we all have different needs to fill, we all have different comfort zones. And the player operating out of his or her comfort zone is not effective. When we operate out of our comfort zone or range, we usually find a way to self -destruct. When an investment doesn't feel right, when it makes us nervous, when we don't understand it—those are probably signs the investment is not for us, and we had better proceed with caution.

We must be realistic about our comfort zones when setting our goals. If we are afraid of debt, if we are unwilling to even consider taking a loss, then we must set our goals lower, or allow more time to achieve them.

4. CREATING THE PLAN

Now that realistic goals have been methodically and thoroughly considered and set in writing, the next step is to construct a plan to implement those goals. The plan must be workable in the player's marketplace. The plan must start with the player's present capabilities, flexibility, involvement and comfort zone. The investor with little or no cash will probably need to plan to be more involved and more flexible than the player with a great deal of cash. The no- or short-cash player will have to invest "sweat equity" and will most assuredly have to start with less desirable properties from the standpoint of location and condition. The heavily involved player's plan may call for that player to trade properties, or acquire properties every year, or even every few months, while the less active player may call for a pyramid step (exchange into a larger property) every three years. Some plans may call for a split of assets, with a portion of the assets being placed in "safe" investments and with other assets earmarked for high-risk/high-return situations.

In creating your plan, ask these questions along each step of the way:

What? Be specific. What do we want to achieve? Define the goals specifically.

When? Establish a firm time schedule for each step and for the ultimate goal.

How? First, we draw on our obvious capabilities and then our imagination. If we want it bad enough, the how will come to us.

How much? What price ranges and equities?

Where? Remember, the more flexible, the better.

Who? What team players will I need? How much help will I require and what can I afford to pay or share?

Why? Reality check. Are the goals really my own?

To be successful, the planner must recognize we do not operate in a vacuum. Our moves will be affected by cycles, innovations, tax laws, politics, financing availability and interest rates as well as fundamental national and global changes caused by such forces as energy shortages, wars, computers, transportation and communication breakthroughs. Basic industries may become obsolete, affecting large numbers of workers, towns, states and countries. Other new industries may spring up, creating glorious opportunities.

These variables should not paralyze the investor with fear, but must be acknowledged and considered in relation to the plan. The plan and planner should be sufficiently flexible to permit appropriate responses. You may also end up revising your plan because your comfort capability, flexibility and involvement will change. BUT YOU NEED A PLAN. Don't be afraid to revise it, but have a plan!

5. ACQUIRING THE FIRST PROPERTY
Don't procrastinate—do it. Don't wait for that once-in-a-lifetime deal—that "real steal." Make the best purchase you can, but do it. Give yourself a deadline—like 90 days. That is plenty of time to find and close on a property. If you can find a competent and eager real estate agent, use him or her. If not, start reading all of the ads for real estate for sale, check the internet, cruise likely neighborhoods looking for "for sale" signs or rundown properties. Learn to use the tax assessor's books (located in the county tax assessor's office and in title company offices) to find the names and addresses of owners.

When you locate the property, make a fair offer based on what you have researched about the values of comparable properties. I always prefer using an agent for negotiating. Principal to principal is the worst way to negotiate. Often, tempers get short and deals get lost because of the personalities involved. An agent can soften the language. Many times, I've had a client say, "tell that jerk to take his deal..." I translate to the other party, "Your offer is unacceptable. Maybe we should try...."

There is a lot of ego in buying and selling real estate. No one wants to think he or she has been taken. Sellers are willing to make a lot more concessions on terms if they can save "face" on the price.

I prefer making offers with contingencies as soon as I think I might be interested in the property. I prefer to get it tied up while I do my "due diligence." The relationship between buyer and seller seems to change after a contract has been signed, from adversarial to cooperative. Once the deal is reached, both parties move together to create the closing.

6. MANAGING THE ASSET

Just as we need an estate-building plan to insure we stay on track buying and exchanging properties, we also need a plan for managing the properties during our ownership. The strategy driving the management plan depends on what we want our properties to achieve for us.

If the goal is to build an estate, and we don't need to take cash from the property, we would develop a management plan that would increase the value of the property to its maximum potential during our period of ownership. We would not be concerned about cash flow beyond its effect on the property's value for the next buyer. This type of management plan might call for us to invest all the cash flow back into property upgrades and to pursue aggressive rent increases.

On the other hand, if we acquire the property because we need the cash flow, then our management plan would set aside the needed cash, with only the surplus going back into the property.

Who manages the property? That will totally depend on the player's capacity. The player whose time is worth several hundred dollars an hour and can afford to go into a larger property would put the property in the care of the best possible professional manager. The player who scraped together a few dollars to get into the property and has a real struggle making ends meet will want to manage the property oneself.

7. PYRAMIDING

Pyramiding is the art or technique of using one's existing assets to acquire more properties. It is an integral part of estate building. A couple, two of my most successful estate builder clients, started their real estate investment career by acquiring an old run-down house for little money (they had very little), renovating it, selling it at a profit, and reinvesting in another. When I met the clients they had a 13-unit apartment and a 16-unit apartment, were developing or acquiring 47 fourplexes and getting ready to start 53 duplexes. I have since exchanged them in, and sometimes out of, shopping centers, offices, rest homes, commercial buildings, land and apartment buildings from coast to coast and border to border. They started with practically no money and now have a net worth well into eight figures.

The basic theory is that when sufficient equity has been built up in a property, either through appreciation, upgrading, or loan pay-down, that equity should be used to acquire bigger properties. Suppose the investor starts with a $200,000 six-unit apartment building, purchased with $40,000 down and a $160,000 loan on the property. As a result of inflation and owner upgrades, the building's worth increases to $300,000 in three years, and the loan is paid down to $155,000. The owner now has $145,000 equity, almost a 50% equity position in the six-plex. If the property were to increase in value 10%, or $30,000 per year, the owner would be receiving 21% on equity due to growth. However, if the owner could move that equity into a $600,000 12-unit building that was also experiencing 10% annual appreciation, then the owner would be receiving $60,000 per year, or a 42% return on equity.

There are three ways to pyramid. The first way is to sell the property, pay a portion of the profit to Uncle Sam in taxes, and then buy a larger property with the residual. The second option is to exchange the equity on a six-unit building for the down payment on a 12-unit building, keeping most of the equity intact (all except commissions and transaction costs). The third method is to retain ownership of the present asset, borrow against the equity (a non-taxable event) and purchase another property with the borrowed funds. In this case, the owner wouldn't go into a 12-unit building, but instead would own two six-unit buildings. This has the added advantage to the estate builder of not having to pay commissions on the sale of the six-plex.

8. REACHING THE GOAL

After pyramiding, the estate builder, if careful and lucky, reaches or exceeds the goal. "Whew, we made it. Net worth two mil. Now what do we do?" Either set new goals or stop. When we stop, the final step is to preserve the estate.

9. PRESERVING THE ESTATE

Preserving the estate takes two forms. The first consideration is not losing the estate to the government in estate taxes. Through the use of family partnerships, installment sales between family members and trusts, much of the estate can be preserved—but only if the preservation plan is implemented while the estate is being built. The estate builder should find a top real estate tax attorney or estate planner and put a plan into motion early in the game.

The second consideration is to prevent losing the assets to recession, money market changes, inflation, economic downturns, vacancies, and other dangers of real property ownership. This should be tackled when the goal has been reached because it requires a complete change of tactics. The player must drop the quest for leverage. No more high-risk, high-return buildings. Now it is time for the safely leased telephone building with cost-of-living increases. Safety is now paramount. Good locations in stable communities with strong tenants are the prime requirements. Let the loans pay down and property appreciate until 50% equity positions are achieving big cash flows. Don't be like a developer acquaintance of mine. He had 24 development projects, and the first 23 were successful. The biggest, the 24th, was not. He is now broke. Instead of remaining in the preservation stage, he reverted to the pyramiding stage.

Enjoy the fruits of playing the real estate game. If still hooked after reaching the goal, take a small portion of the estate and play with that. Don't cross-collateralize, using one asset to guarantee another, and don't personally guarantee loans by allowing your real estate to be the security on a new loan. Keep the "play real estate" completely separate from the "achieved estate."

Chapter 11
The Team

The investor needs a quality team to insure optimum results. Ultimately, the team will consist of the real estate broker, the legal advisor, the tax advisor, the property manager and the escrow officer (or closing attorney). At the embryonic stages of the investment program, especially if the investor is operating with little capital, he or she might forego the tax and legal advisor and property manager, instead relying on his or her own knowledge in those areas. The investor might also find a transaction that is for sale by owner and decide to negotiate it personally. However, if the investor is serious and intends to use real estate as an estate building vehicle, he or she should begin to assemble the finest team available to assist in those efforts and use that team transaction after transaction, year after year. It is very possible that the team will mean the difference between success and failure in achieving the investor's goals.

THE BROKER

The job of the real estate broker is to find the best property available—one that meets the investor's requirements and is within the investor's capabilities—negotiate the purchase and assist in the closing.

An outstanding broker will do much more. The outstanding broker will first counsel with the client and determine the client's long- and short-term goals, capabilities and fears, ambitions and abilities, strengths and weaknesses, hobbies and talents, and then design an investment program that will take the investor from the present position to the desired goals. This broker may assist with the plan, advising the estate builder what is possible and practical. He or she will coordinate with the tax and legal advisors and assist the escrow officer or closing attorney in completing the transaction. This broker will follow up. He or she will provide or coordinate the property management. During the negotiation stages, he or she will design the transaction to meet the investor's needs and capabilities. This broker will have knowledge of the tax laws affecting real estate, including depreciation, tax-deferred exchanges, installment sales, capital contributions to corporations and partnerships, dealer and investor activities and have knowledge of estate planning, including family partnerships and trusts. The outstanding broker will not be as complete in his or her knowledge of these areas as the investor's tax advisor, but will have sufficient knowledge to plan strategy.

The outstanding investment broker will know the investment market, locally, regionally and nationally, and have a feeling for trends. No broker is infallible, and the ultimate decision remains with the investor, but the broker should be able to have an intelligent discussion of the pros and cons of each investment. He or she should access a database of available properties, provide property comparisons and analyze the income and tax ramifications of various transactions. He or she may belong to a network of investment brokers nationally and have access to investments and information throughout the country.

What are the qualities that are important in choosing a broker? In order of importance:

HONESTY: The broker that lies, misrepresents, omits or is fraudulent can bring losses, lawsuits and emotional devastation that will sour the investor forever on real estate. If there is any question about the broker's integrity, ask for and check out references—or just walk away.

KNOWLEDGE: Most brokers are not investment brokers. Most are residential brokers. Undoubtedly, if the first investment is a house or a duplex, a residential broker will not only suffice, but will be the most knowledgeable in that area. However, when the investor gets beyond homes for investment, then an investment broker should be retained.

WILLINGNESS TO WORK: Locating an honest and knowledgeable broker will be to no avail if the broker is unwilling to spend the time needed to get the job done. A high-earning investment broker will work smart rather than long and will use the modern methods and contacts to get results. If the broker is not bringing in transactions, he or she is not working. Conversely, if the investor rejects all transactions that the knowledgeable broker presents, the broker will lose the incentive to work for that investor.

LOYALTY: Top brokers expect and demand loyalty, and clients should demand the same loyalty in return. The ideal synergy exists when the broker prioritizes the client's interests and the client always works through the broker.

WILLINGNESS TO COOPERATE AND CONTACTS: The broker who will not cooperate with other brokers and doesn't have contacts throughout the community, region or country limits the number of investments available to the investor and the number of takers available for the investor's properties.

COMPATIBILITY: Hopefully the relationship between broker and investor will be long and profitable for both parties. Over time, problems will inevitably arise. However, if there is a basic compatibility, problems can be worked out. Besides, it is more fun to work with people you like.

BUYER BROKERAGE

In the past, a major conflict has haunted the brokerage community. The broker retained by the buyer-investor to assist in locating and closing the acquisition of a property is usually paid, indirectly, by the seller. The listing broker, hired by the seller, splits the commission with the "cooperating" broker. Indirectly, the buyer's broker is being paid by the seller.

This has long been the custom but it has created two problems

First, from a legal standpoint, there is an agency problem. The investor's broker is really representing one party, the buyer, while being paid by the "opponent," the seller. In California, this seems to have been resolved by ensuring all parties are informed as to each broker's functions and responsibilities. Real estate sales contracts and agency disclosure forms are now part of all standard forms and educational requirements and the paying party no longer seems to be a prime issue.

The second problem is financial and cannot be resolved so easily. Some sellers are willing to pay only 2% commissions while others will pay up to 10%, and while some brokers are willing to take listings at whatever the owner is willing to pay, most top professionals are not. The conflict comes when the buyer's broker is searching out properties for a client and is presented two properties, one of which will pay the broker a $5,000 commission and the other a $30,000 commission. If the buyer's broker is being paid by the seller he or she may be reluctant to even present the first property, although it may better serve the client's plan and goals.

One resolution is buyer brokerage. The broker and client have a BUYER'S BROKERAGE CONTRACT, also called a "single agency contract," which provides that the broker will receive an amount equal to a certain percentage of the value of the property acquired (3%, 6% or whatever they agree on). This sum is paid by the investor, the party the broker is truly representing. The property should be acquired at a lower price to reflect the fact that the seller is not paying the full commission to both the listing and buyer's brokers.

COUNSELING

In the traditional client-broker relationship the client tells the broker what he or she wants and then the broker attempts to locate property or buyer. An alternative method of initiating the relationship, and often a much more profitable course of action for both parties, is the counseling approach. The counseling approach begins with the broker and potential client spending time discussing the client's goals, resources, family, comfort and discomfort zones, as well as the broker's method of operation and fees. Usually there is no charge for this first session. Some counselors tape all meetings, others take notes.

This first meeting will close with one of these results:
1) The broker, client, or both decide they each don't want to work with the other, and there will be no further meeting.
2) The client-applicant and broker decide another meeting is in order before committing to move ahead.
3) They agree to work together with the broker acting as a consultant on an hourly fee basis.
4) The broker and client decide to work together with the broker being paid on a contingency (commissions) basis.

If they decide to work together, the broker and client will enter into a contract for the broker to represent the client. The contract may provide for a retainer. Some professionals charge an hourly fee which will be credited against commissions. The contract usually provides a 30-day cancellation clause.

The professional broker will require that the client assist in the marketing effort, including paying for a preliminary title report if the client is selling or exchanging a property, as well as providing income and expense figures, maps, pictures and any other property information he or she might have on file. The broker will also require property and personal financial information, including financial statements and tax returns. The broker will then be able to analyze possible tax implications and measure after tax yields for all potential transactions.

The estate building investor should search carefully for the broker to represent him or her, and then, as long as the broker performs, remain absolutely loyal to that broker. A top investment broker can make an investor millions, providing the investor is flexible and has the daring to make the necessary moves.

How does the investor find a top investment broker? Top professional designations include:

S.E.C.—The most creative brokers in the country are members of the National Society of Exchange Counselors. Less than 125 in number, these highly screened and experienced professionals are generally independent and own their own brokerage houses. Members have offices in all sections of the United States. A member of the Society of Exchange Counselors is identified by S.E.C. following the broker's name.

CCIM—The highest professional designation for investment brokers approved by the National Association of Realtors is Certified Commercial Investment Member, and the letters CCIM following the broker's name denotes that the broker has achieved that designation. To become a CCIM, an agent must be experienced, have completed extensive courses, passed rigorous examinations, and demonstrated and verified that he or she has structured and closed elaborate investment transactions. CCIMs are listed on-line, and information regarding members may be obtained through the National Association of Realtors, Chicago, Illinois.

EMS—The designation for an Equity Marketing Specialist, those agents who have passed the Gold Card Course from the National Council of Exchangors.

Other qualified brokers include those listed in the annual publication, *Who's Who of Creative Real Estate*, and those who hold G.R.I. (Graduate Realtor's Institute) designations.

The investment divisions of the larger national companies, (CB Commercial, Cushman-Wakefield, Grubb & Ellis, etc.) employ some very talented people, many of whom are extremely qualified specialists.

A designation or employment by a big house does not necessarily guarantee the investor is getting the best brokerage talent available, but is a good place to start. The investor should anticipate working with the broker for years or even decades and should choose the individual for the long haul.

THE LEGAL ADVISOR

At the early stages of an estate building career, most investors use their personal attorney. Unfortunately, many continue to do so long after that attorney is out of his or her element. Attorneys specialize. Even amongst real estate attorneys there are experts in specific areas such as subdivisions, syndication, development and taxation.

As an investment broker, developer, syndicator, exchanger and an investor who has used attorneys in all of the above functions, I have formed some strong opinions on the best ways to work with legal counsel. First, I have a real estate specialist who is my general practitioner. He is very bright and an outstanding detail person who has more "what ifs?" than anybody I ever met. That is a very important qualification for any attorney—one who thinks of all of the "what ifs" that you may have missed. My attorney is also totally thorough in reviewing or drafting a contract. And, he is available. Often my real estate transaction cannot survive a week's delay waiting for an attorney to return a phone call or review a document. But this is not the same attorney I use for tax advice, nor for condominium development or syndication work. I use legal specialists in those areas. Because these specialists know their subject thoroughly, I don't have to pay for them to research cases or hit the law-books.

I use attorneys whom I consider deal-makers, not deal-killers. Marvin Starr, whom I consider to be the brightest and most creative real estate tax attorney in the country, is the epitome of a deal-maker. There are times when I run up against a stone wall mentally in some complex exchange. Within 30 minutes, Marv can provide several solutions that either I had overlooked or had not yet been invented.

When counseling with a prospective client, one of my questions is, "Do you have third parties that assist you with your decisions?" If their attorney is such a party, I insist on meeting with the attorney (or any other third party influence) to determine whether we will be able to work together. If we are unable to agree on the objectives and methods, I will not take on the applicant as a client. One of my biggest problems with attorneys is when they offer investment advice rather than legal advice.

When involved in larger transactions, attorneys are an absolute necessity. The bottom line is: use a specialist, a deal-maker, not a deal-killer, and one who is available.

THE TAX ADVISOR

The tax advisor is generally a Certified Public Accountant (CPA), a tax attorney or a Public Accountant (PA). The complexity and size of the transaction will determine the degree of skill needed by the tax advisor. A multimillion dollar potential tax liability needs greater care in planning than one involving a thousand dollars. Many ex-IRS agents are practicing accountants, and many top tax people regularly visit both professionally and socially with their counterparts in the "service."

Like attorneys, accountants specialize. The skills of team members need to keep pace with the estate builder. If they don't, changes will need to be made. As the player's real estate portfolio grows in size and complexity, it becomes increasingly important to upgrade the level of professional talent.

THE ESCROW OFFICER AND CLOSING ATTORNEY

I have never used a closing attorney because I broker in California where we use escrow officers. Escrow officers are trained professionals who work for escrow or title companies and whose only job (typically) is to hold and close real estate escrows.

A real estate escrow is the independent agency where the buyer places the purchase funds and the seller places the deed to the property. When all of the "conditions" of the escrow are met and the funds and deed are delivered to the other party, it's called an "escrow closing." That is the simple definition, but in reality escrow closings are not usually simple because the conditions of closing are not simple.

A typical escrow closing condition is that the buyer receives good title (proof of ownership) to the property. Over the centuries, proof of good title has evolved into California's system of "title insurance," where a large, strong financial institution writes an insurance policy, insuring that the title being passed to the buyer is, in fact, the good and marketable property ownership. Most states, and other countries, have followed California's lead and title insurance is widely available.

Often the real estate lender becomes a party to the escrow. A buyer will obtain a new loan or assume an existing loan to finance the property's purchase. The lender will only place a loan on the property if they know that the security (the property) has good title and that the borrower has the right to use the property as security.

An entire book could be written (and probably has) about escrows. My experience is that the escrow officer is one of the most critical team members and his or her ability to work through and solve problems often makes the difference between a transaction's success and failure.

Most of my big, complicated exchanges would not have closed without the talented escrow officers I have used. I have also had the misfortune of being a defendant in a lawsuit as a result of an incompetent escrow officer's mistakes.

I assume closing attorneys (which are used in some other states) are like escrow officers, in that some are more qualified, more creative, more open-minded, and more reliable than others.

I usually demand to choose the escrow officer. When I use my escrow officer, he/she will keep me posted if something strange comes up. And, I know the escrow is in good hands. I will make an exception when I am dealing with another broker that I highly respect and that broker feels even more strongly about their escrow officer than I do. The trade-off is that if I agree to use their escrow officer, the other broker must be willing to do most of the closing work.

THE PROPERTY MANAGER

After the purchase, the success or failure of the investment is dependent upon how the property is managed. Property management can be divided into two types: on-site and off-site.

Apartment buildings, mobile home parks and large self storage units require on-site managers. This is not necessarily a legal requirement, but good business practice. The on-site manager shows vacancies, handles maintenance problems, may collect rents and generally represents the owner in the day-to-day interaction with the tenants.

Without an on-site manager, the property owner may soon weary of the calls to show a unit or handle a leaking faucet. Even in the case of a duplex, I prefer to give one of the two tenants a minor rent concession to be responsible for small repairs and showings.

The on-site manager is supervised by the off-site manager. The off-site manager surveys the competition, creates a management plan, sets the rents and rental terms, creates and implements an operating budget, hires and fires on-site management, sets up a cadre of maintenance people and interacts with the owner.

Initially, the small property owner will probably be the off-site manager. When the investment grows too large or time consuming, the alternative is the professional property management company.

Professional property management firms are located in every community in the United States and their competency varies from outstanding to abysmal. The outstanding firm will have a management plan and budget that it will actively and aggressively follow, with the objective being to keep the owner's property full of quality tenants at the highest possible rents. The firm will maintain the property in an excellent condition with a well-trained on-site staff while keeping the budget intact. This firm will know the competition, their strengths and weaknesses. The on-site people will "sell" the tenants on why they should occupy your building. And they will know the laws affecting tenants and landlords rights.

It is good practice for the owner to interview several professional management firms. Each firm should submit a proposal, a list of references and a financial statement. The references should be checked out.

Some firms place a surcharge on outside contractor's maintenance work, while others charge extra for leasing vacancies. These variables must be clarified before signing a property management contract.

Management fees typically run from around 10% on houses and small units to as low as 3% on large apartment complexes. On-site costs are usually in addition to the off-site management cost.

When I have moved I have searched for new, qualified people to work with. I like working with local people as different locations have different traditions. In some counties, it is traditional for the seller to pay for the title insurance. In others, the buyer pays. In some areas, the contract goes directly into escrow and the escrow instructions become the guiding document. In other locations, escrow isn't even opened until all due diligence is done and the closing is imminent. When looking for a new team member, I start by asking every real estate professional that I respect who they use and why. This is effective when attempting to locate escrow people, tax attorneys, accountants, lenders, and any other team members.

In choosing any team, it is important to work with people you like. Putting real estate deals together can be great fun—or can be a very demanding chore. Working with a team you like and respect will result in your making more and better transactions.

Chapter 12
Comparative Investments

In boom times or bust, the investor has a wide selection from which to choose a property to purchase for an investment. He or she can choose houses, condos, duplexes, apartments, commercial, industrial, offices, mobile home parks, self-storage warehouses, farms, ranches or bare land. The investor can go it alone or in partnership with others. Partners can be chosen because of their expertise or their ability to invest dollars. The investor can hold for appreciation or buy, upgrade and sell or exchange. He/she can buy existing properties or develop new properties for even bigger profits. The variety seems endless. In order to understand the benefits each property might offer, we will group the properties with common characteristics.

As discussed in the timing section, some property groups are riskier, while others have more overall stability. In 2010, when the future of most investment real estate is of concern, the investor must think through what properties will be needed in the years to come. What is the impact of the mobility provided by laptop computers, iPhones and tele-conferencing? Will office buildings remain necessary? What impact will on-line shopping have on retail? There are millions of square feet of vacant industrial space. Will it ever fill? Will hotels regain their pre-recession weekday occupancy rates, or will other avenues of communication slow the business traveler?

I believe all of the above will have an effect. But, we still need to know the fundamentals.

THE GROWTH/TAX SHELTER GROUP—Properties in this group consist of single family residences, condominiums, duplexes and small apartment buildings. The common thread in this group is their generally lower than average before-tax yields, with the primary reasons for ownership being growth and tax shelter.

THE GROWTH/YIELD GROUP—Properties in this group consist of large apartment buildings, commercial and industrial office buildings, self-storage warehouses, and mobile home parks. They are purchased for yield as well as growth.

THE YIELD GROUP—Paper (loans secured by real estate) and long-term fixed lease properties are usually purchased for yield only.

THE GROWTH GROUP—Land. Land generally has no yield, but can provide the fastest of all growth opportunities.

THE BUSINESS GROUP— Properties in this group include hotels, motels, development projects, and conversions. Although technically real estate, they are businesses and must be run as such.

The following is a look at these individual investment groups.

THE GROWTH/TAX SHELTER GROUP
SINGLE FAMILY RESIDENCES
Investment houses are purchased for future growth and present-day tax shelter. They do not bring big cash flows. Houses offer good tax shelter (when available) because of their high improvement-to-land ratio and relatively short economic life.

Houses are a good pyramiding vehicle. Being the easiest to finance and sell, they are the most liquid (convertible to cash). There are more buyers for houses than any other type of real estate.

In recent memory, houses were relatively low risk prior to the crash of 2006-08. Well-located single family residences rarely lost more than 5% of their value. Most homeowners didn't need to sell, which stabilized the market. However, sub-prime loans and 100% financing kicked the props out from under the inflated single family and condo markets. While we all felt the impact of cascading home prices, it must be recognized that the giant losses were only realized on the very inflated gains of the previous five years. The very depressed housing market had dropped to 2002 prices and probably would have stabilized if not for absurd lending practices and speculator greed.

Buying a well-located home or condo at depressed prices can be the smartest and safest investment around.

The big risk in any investment—being buried in an unwanted commodity and unable to liquidate—is less in houses more than in any other real estate group because of the broad homebuyer and lender market. But the investor must be able to afford to feed a negative cash flow if a property is vacant.

Single family residences are the most easily financed of all real estate. Loans of 75% to 97% of value are available on houses, a higher loan-to-value percentage than is available on any other type of real estate investment.

Houses require a fair amount of property management, but this can be mitigated by careful tenant screening and large security deposits.

Before buying an investment house, the following should be determined:
a) the trend of the house market;
b) the growth of the community;

c) area acceptability (i.e. high crime areas);

d) the financing potential of the property;

e) the replacement cost;

f) the rental market; and

g) comparable prices.

Houses are one of the best investments for the starter investor. They are financially easy to get into and on an individual basis, do not require too much management. They are low risk, a great pyramiding vehicle, and a good management training ground. Although low yield, in a good market they can be outstanding growth investments.

CONDOMINIUMS

Condominiums basically have the same characteristics as single family residences; they are a growth investment with limited yield, offering some tax shelter. They can be an excellent pyramiding vehicle, usually offering relatively low risk. They require less management than houses because the exterior is maintained as part of the common area. Additional considerations in condo investments are the common area agreement, the association's financial condition, the homeowner's fees, and the conditions, covenants, and restrictions (CC&Rs).

APARTMENT BUILDINGS

Most small (2-4 units) apartment buildings in the Western United States are growth investments and offer only moderate yields. For example, if you buy an apartment building at 8 to 12 times gross scheduled income, with 40% expenses and a 5% vacancy, the cap rate at 8 times gross is 6.7%, and at 12 times gross is 4.6%—a yield well below many other investments. However, if the same property can be purchased at six times the scheduled gross, the property will have a 9.5% cap rate, comparable to many commercial properties.

Apartments offer some tax shelter. They have good land-to-improvement ratios, a relative short life and leverage. They are also good pyramiding vehicles. They are salable and relatively easy to finance. Up to 75%

loan-to-value financing is possible for apartment houses, and often money is available for apartment loans when funds for other investment properties have dried up.

Compared to commercial, industrial, and office buildings, apartments are not especially risky. There is an ongoing demand for housing, and vacancies, when they do occur, are usually a much smaller percentage of the entire project. One vacancy in a 12 unit apartment is only eight percent of the complex while a major tenant vacating a shopping center can leave 50% or more of the space without income.

Additional risks in owning apartment houses include rent controls, problem tenants and changing tax laws. Beware of purchasing apartment buildings or single family residences at a price above their replacement costs. Small apartments require intensive management. Owners of larger apartment houses are usually able to afford professional management.

Apartments are especially attractive to the active estate building investor. They are more predicable than commercial properties, and when the tenant improvements are computed into commercial property proformas, they offer nearly as attractive a yield.

Low risk, good returns, good pyramiding, and available financing are all factors that combine to make apartment buildings some of the best investment opportunities. Management headaches are the major drawback.

THE GROWTH/YIELD GROUP
LEASES:
The financial safety and income of commercial and industrial properties, office buildings and shopping centers are so dependent on leases that prior to exploring the investments themselves we will review some common leasing terms.

LEASE TYPES:

Gross Lease: The landlord pays all of the property expenses, including the taxes, insurance, management, maintenance, repairs and in the case of office buildings, even janitorial.

Net Net Net Lease: This is also called a "triple net lease" and sometimes just a "net lease." The tenant pays all of the property expenses including the taxes, insurance, management, maintenance, repairs and janitorial. Typically the landlord would pay for repairs to the roof and outside walls.

Many leases have terms that range between gross and triple net and provide for the tenant to pay some expenses and the landlord pay the balance. These leases have no consistent industry-wide name.

Percentage Leases: A lease in which a tenant not only is obligated to pay a base ("minimum") rent, but also pays a percentage of their income (usually gross income) to the landlord as rent for their space.

OTHER LEASE TERMS:

Credit Tenant: They are also called "national tenants." These tenants are so strong financially that a lender will loan on a property just because this strong financial entity is obligated on a lease to pay rent.

Cost of Living Increases: Also called COLs and CPIs, for Consumer Price Index or Increases. Properties leased to non-retail tenants will usually provide for cost of living increases to ensure the property's real income will not deteriorate with inflation. These COLs are tied to any one of several "indexes," such as the Consumer Price Index.

Common Area Maintenance: Multi-tenant commercial properties share certain common areas such as bathrooms, hallways and/or parking lots. It is quite common for the tenants to share the costs for all or part of this "common area maintenance" (CAM). Each tenant's CAM responsibility is outlined in one's lease.

LENGTH OF LEASES:

Income property leases will typically have terms from one to twenty years, with three to five years being the norm. Anything less than three years would be considered short-term and anything over five years would be considered long-term.

COMMERCIAL & SHOPPING CENTERS

Commercial buildings and shopping centers are yield investments with growth potential that varies from poor to outstanding, depending on the leases. Properties with a fixed income over a long period, without percentage leases or provisions for cost of living increases, may actually lose value over the term of their leases. Owning a commercial building with good percentage leases or cost of living increases can be an outstanding growth investment, taking advantage of either inflation or a tenant's increased sales volume.

Commercial properties and shopping centers have traditionally been one of the best yield investments. Cap rates range from 6-8% when dealing with a triple net leased building to a credit tenant, to 12-13% or more if renting to less credit-worthy tenants on short-term leases.

With stores going "dark" and tenants re-negotiating rents downward, shopping center owners are in deep trouble, and the value of centers is plunging. Credit tenants are going broke. To make matters worse, many shopping center loans are coming due, and with higher vacancies and market uncertainty, appraisers are valuing centers much lower while lenders are requiring higher loan-to-value ratios. Loans are being called, with no replacement financing available. In 2010, the players in this market are the Vulture Funds, circling on wounded and dying real estate investments.

Shopping centers as tax shelters generally fall short compared to houses, apartment buildings, or office buildings because of their poor land/improvement ratio and longer economic life. Land zoned for commercial use is often the most expensive real estate, and sometimes represents

50% or more of the total value of the property creating a high ratio of land costs to improvements.

As a pyramiding vehicle, shopping centers rate about the same as office buildings, and are somewhat less desirable than houses and apartment buildings. To pyramid generally requires takers for the presently owned property and there just aren't as many knowledgeable buyers nor brokers for commercial properties. Most brokers understand houses and apartments, but many never become comfortable with leases and leasing, a key to successful commercial, office building, and industrial investments.

The risk in commercial property ownership is almost entirely dependent upon the tenants and their leases. A building triple-net leased to a major credit tenant can be an extremely safe investment, if the credit tenant remains a credit tenant. Buildings with large spaces rented to poor credit tenants, who are liable to vacate or go broke, are rife with danger and place the investor in a very precarious position. Due diligence prior to buying is of paramount importance.

Normally, financing commercial properties is dependent upon the tenant(s) and the financial market. In 2010, banks are not making commercial loans. Even if they wanted to, the regulators are preventing it. There have been times that with a good, strong tenant, 100% financing has been possible. When a property is leased to weak, local tenants and has a history of vacancies, financing is difficult, expensive, and sometimes impossible. Lenders will generally not commit to a loan in excess of 75% of the purchase price or appraisal, whichever is less, and will want to see a debt coverage ratio between 1.05% and 1.25%.

The amount of management required depends on the property and leases and can vary from nearly none to intensive. The term "coupon clipper," borrowed from the stock market, applies to those triple-net leased, single credit tenant buildings about which all passive investors dream. Owning a building where the owner's total responsibility is to pick up the rent check each month and deposit it in the bank makes this type of commercial the most management-free of all real estate investments.

However, much commercial is quite management intensive. Imagine owning a mall where the owner not only has to perform all of the management functions required in apartment buildings, but also operate a tenant association.

As to expenses, the lease spells out the rent including overage, percentage and cost of living increases, what portion of the common area maintenance the tenant will pay and whether the tenant will pay the taxes, insurance and other costs to maintain the property. The investor must carefully study the leases before committing to the purchase of a commercial building.

OFFICE BUILDINGS

Office buildings are yield investments with growth potential, but they are very volatile as to growth. When office buildings are overbuilt, and they often are, they seem impossible to market. When they are in short supply, their value rises rapidly. Usually they sell at a higher cap rate and thus bring a greater return than apartment buildings. Depending on whether it is a buyers' or sellers' market, the location, the tenants and the leases, office buildings sell at cap rates from 6% to 12%.

As a tax shelter, they rate relatively high. They can have a good land/improvement ratio, although this is partially offset by their long economic life.

Office buildings are high risk because of their historic cyclical over-building and resultant high vacancy factors. Tenants also have a tendency to move from older, more out-dated office buildings (called B & C buildings) to newer, more modern ones (A buildings), which results in high vacancies, lower rents and poorer tenants in older buildings. To reduce risk, new buildings should be pre-leased prior to construction or well-leased if buying an existing building.

The exception to this advice is when a distressed office building can be purchased for pennies on the dollar and successfully renovated. These are not projects for amateurs.

Office buildings are more difficult to finance than houses or apartment buildings, but still easier than unimproved real estate. They are not as salable as houses or apartment buildings because there are not as many buyers who understand office building risk and management.

Offices can require intensive or little management depending on the type of leases and the services demanded by the tenants. Single tenant offices are easier to manage than apartments or houses.

When investing in office buildings it is important to monitor the office building market conditions. Most of the major commercial brokerage houses maintain local demographics, including present vacancies, absorption rates and the amount of square footage coming on line. If possible, locate a city where office buildings are nearly full, where there will be a future space shortage and where there are no new office building construction starts. This will provide the optimum opportunity for growth.

Office building investments are for the experienced real estate professional.

INDUSTRIAL & RESEARCH AND DEVELOPMENT (R&D) BUILDINGS

Industrial buildings are yield investments with growth potential. As with commercial and office buildings, growth is dependent upon the length of the leases, whether they provide for cost of living increases, the type and strength of tenants, and the property location.

The cap rate on industrial properties is relatively high—7% to 12% and sometimes even higher. The actual yield depends on the same factors as growth potential. Remember, the safer the investment, the lower the yield.

Industrial buildings offer about the same tax shelter as commercial properties.

The risk in industrial property ownership depends on the tenant and the supply and demand for space in the area. Short-term leases, obsolete buildings, and mobile tenants create high risk. Well-funded tenants on long leases, with a great deal of their own capital invested in the building's tenant improvements, usually indicate lower risk, as do properties in markets with few vacancies and high demand.

Financing of industrial and R & D properties was, and again will be, dependent on the leases and tenants' strength. With a prime tenant and a favorable financing market, 75% to 80% and even higher loan-to-value financing on industrial buildings is available, generally through insurance companies.

Industrial buildings normally require little management. Leases commonly run from three to ten years, some of them with renewal options.

Good locations are those near other industrial properties, with good highway access. Most new industrial buildings are located in industrial parks. The most desirable industrial buildings have ceiling heights of 18 to 22 feet and higher.

What type of investor should consider investing in industrial buildings? Institutional investors are prime candidates for well-leased, single-tenant industrial buildings, but smaller single- and multi-tenant buildings can be good profit centers for the aggressive investor who is willing to do some leasing work when vacancies occur. My brother, certainly no big hitter, became an early retiree through ownership of several small industrial buildings.

SELF-STORAGE (MINI) WAREHOUSES
There are two basic types of warehouses; those with large spaces used by industrial firms, and small, multi-tenant, self-storage units. Large,

industrial type warehouses are similar to industrial buildings, and the same criteria and analyses apply.

Self-storage warehouses are a different type of industrial property entirely. Physically, the buildings incorporate a series of small spaces for the use of individuals and businesses.

These investments can offer excellent appreciation as the tenants are all on short-term leases or month-to-month tenancy, which easily allows for rental increases when market conditions or inflation dictates. Self-storage warehouses have a great deal in common with large apartment complexes in that they cater to a large number of small tenants with short-term tenancy agreements. Unlike commercial or industrial, where the leases determine the value of the investment, the upside potential, the risk and the financing potential, self-storage warehouse profitability is closely tied to the immediate supply and demand of the market.

Location and visibility are extremely important. A very successful self-storage warehouse developer warned never to buy a property where a competitor can get between you and your market.

Self-storage warehouses are very difficult to finance. Historically, some savings and loan associations and banks have financed them, but often only up to 50% of their value. Private, hard money lenders are the expensive alternative. Obviously, poor financing hampers liquidity and the ability of the owner to pyramid.

In California, self-storage warehouses sell at around an 8-10% cap rate, and in much of the United States, 12% or higher.

As tax shelters, they rate somewhat low because of the poor land/improvement ratio.

Self-storage warehouses require intensive management. As much as 20-50% of the spaces vacate and re-rent during a month. This necessitates checking people in and out, and ensuring the spaces are clean and well maintained. For that reason and for reasons of security, large self-storage warehouses have managers living on the premises. One of the manager's perks is free housing.

The major risk in self-storage warehouse ownership is overbuilding. As with other profitable investments, when competitors see a booming market and handsome profits, they want a piece of the pie. The main deterrent to overbuilding is the financing problem.

Self-storage warehouses, in areas where they are not overbuilt, can make outstanding investments for the investor or group who has the cash to handle a large equity requirement.

THE GROWTH GROUP
LAND
Land can be divided into four classifications:
1. Development land—land that is ready or nearly ready to build upon.
2. Predevelopment land—land that will be ready to develop within one to five years.
3. Warehouse land—land which is only held for investment and has no productive use or near-term potential (i.e. dry mountain or desert land).
4. Farm or ranch land.

Land that is not purchased by a user is usually purchased for growth because land, unless it is developed, leased out, or used for farming or ranching, has no yield.

Land is a very poor tax shelter investment. The only tax advantage in owning land is that the taxes and the interest payments are deductible. True tax shelter in real estate is through the paper depreciation of buildings, and with land this does not exist. By planting trees or vines on land, you can create depreciation and investment tax credits, if they are available under the current tax law.

Land is a poor pyramiding vehicle unless it is development land with a developer waiting to buy. In this unique case, the investor will have cash to acquire another "like" property using a 1031 exchange.

Land offers no risk as long as the investor is prepared to make the payments and pay taxes during the holding period.

Land is very difficult to finance institutionally. Historically, land lenders are previous owners (sellers) carrying back a loan on their own property. Often they are willing to do so as this is the only way that they can sell their property.

Land requires very little management, but don't be mistaken—it does require some. Someone has to pay the taxes and insurance, go to the zoning meetings and be responsible for maintaining it so it is not a danger to others.

Considering all the negatives, why would anyone invest in land? It is quite simple. Land can offer the greatest growth of any type of investment and, historically, has. There are thousands of cases where land value near cities has doubled, tripled or increased tenfold in just a few years. Likely more fortunes have been made in land development and speculation that in any other type of real estate investment.

I love land. I have a wonderful time walking a potential subdivision or homesite. Laying out streets and brainstorming a higher and better use for a land parcel is heady work.

But land development certainly has its risks. Important considerations include: Will the environmentalists and government permit development of the land? Will utilities come to the site? Will there still be a market for what I plan for the property when I finally get all the approvals necessary to move ahead? This is huge. Many developers have crashed because of the lead time needed to entitle and develop a property. Where it once took weeks to create an approved subdivision, now it can take years, during which time the market can (and has) turned.

All real estate, but particularly land, can be either a speculative investment or one where additional value is created. By improving, zoning, receiving entitlements, or subdividing, value can be enhanced without actually disturbing the land. Grading, clearing and planting can physically enhance land value. Creating plans or a better use for the property are other value enhancements.

THE BUSINESS GROUP
HOTELS AND MOTELS

Hotels and motels are not an investment as much as they are a business opportunity. They can be considered an investment only if they are purchased and leased to an operator on an absolutely net basis. In most cases, however, motels are owned by users, and they are clearly businesses.

Hotels/motels require good locations and sound business practices to be profitable. Income and growth depend on how well they are managed and operated. Well managed motels and hotels can make excellent profits.

They offer excellent tax shelter opportunities because of the high improvement/land ratio and the extensive personal property investments which allow for tax credits and short-term life depreciation. Often, there are business tax advantages available in hotels/motels, not otherwise found in traditional investment real estate. Current IRS policies should be reviewed with an investor's CPA.

Hotels and motels are very high risk. It is often a cash business, with a cash business's inherent temptations; thus, it is imperative that the owner have good controls in place.

Financing is very poor, and often nonexistent except for owner carry-back financing (seller taking a note for a portion of the purchase price).

Management is critical. Someone must be taking an active interest on a daily basis.

The ideal type of investor for a hotel or motel is an experienced user/operator or an active group.

DEVELOPMENT

There is more wealth potential through developing than any other single type of real estate opportunity. Probably nowhere, in any industry, are fortunes made as quickly as by the real estate developer. Millions are made each year by developers, many without a great deal of education, but with nerve, the ability to see a profit in a project, and the willingness to take the risk and spend the time to make the project work.

It is not a piece of cake. The developer must do his/her homework thoroughly: checking the market to determine what is "on stream," in the planning stages to be built, how long the market is going to last, whether the community can support the development, whether financing is available, and whether or not it can be rented, leased, or sold for a price sufficient to make it a profitable venture. The developer must be prepared to fight obstructionists and NIMBYs (Not In My BackYard), and to spend long hours at planning and counseling meetings being insulted by people never before met. And the developer must be prepared to lose on occasions. There are no sure things.

There are two reasons for development: to sell at a profit; or to hold for income producing purposes. Developing for a profit offers tremendous immediate income benefits. There is no tax shelter in developing to sell, because the tax shelter would pass on to the buyer and the developer would be a "dealer" in relation to that property.

Developing to hold for income producing purposes is an outstanding estate building tool. This can offer abnormal appreciation because the developer/holder/owner is taking the developer's profit, which can run as high as 25% of the value of the building, in addition to the normal real estate benefits. The yield then becomes extremely high based upon investment, considerably higher than most other investments.

The risk is high in developing because the developer faces numerous variables: market shift; city, county, state, and federal governments; Coastal Commissions; environmentalists and other special interest groups; money markets that can cause the availability of money to go from readily available to "sorry, we are out of funds"; and tenants who may become unavailable, in the midst of construction. Every time a variable is added, risk is increased.

Financing can vary from poor to outstanding. In 2010, it is virtually unavailable to all except the most liquid borrowers. The historic, and much dreamt of, 100% loans in good money markets may still be possible, somewhere in the future. But, more realistically, lenders will eventually resume lending, on sound projects, an amount equal to 75% of value or 80% of costs, whichever is less.

The three necessary ingredients for real estate development are capital, a strong financial statement, and expertise in developing; none of which the developer has to have oneself. Nor does the developer have to be a contractor. The role of a developer is basically that of a coordinating, decision-making principal. The developer can contract with all of his/ her team members, including the contractor, and I'm not aware of any license requirement for development in any state.

Management during the construction period is quite intensive. After completion, management needs would depend upon the type of development.

As in all real estate investments, special consideration must be given to location when developing. Design, pride of ownership, low maintenance, and the ability to obtain sufficient financing are all critical considerations, but equally important is the attitude of the principal. Developing is not a game for the easily discouraged, or faint of heart. Wimps need not apply!

CONVERSIONS

A conversion takes place when the property owner changes the property's function or legal status. Conversions are now quite commonplace with apartment houses being converted to condominiums, gas stations to flower shops, warehouses to office buildings, and office buildings to office condos.

Conversions are for an active investor. They have the same problems and offer the same large profits as development projects. Most conversions are not long-term investments, but are done for short-term profits. This may have adverse tax consequences for the converter, as the profits may be taxed as ordinary income. A market and feasibility study must be conducted prior to embarking on a conversion.

Important conversion team members are attorneys and structural engineers. Make sure the local governmental agencies will allow your conversion before you purchase the property you wish to convert.

RENOVATIONS (REHABS, FIXER-UPPERS)

Like conversions, fixer-uppers require an active investor. Many people have made fortunes purchasing run-down buildings, renovating them, and selling them at a profit. The level of risk depends upon the investor's financial capability to complete the project, in spite of the common, and sometimes considerable, cost overruns inherent in most construction jobs. Hidden costs lurk behind every wall—asbestos cries to be removed, faulty wiring and dry rot await. It's prudent to have a substantial short term line of credit at the bank or a heavyweight financial partner ready to assist.

The market must be checked to insure there is sufficient demand for the finished product and that the project will show a profit. A profit/loss analysis must be run on these types of investments before starting.

The renovation investor is a developer/activist with the financial resources to carry the project through to completion.

Chapter 13
Property Acquisition in Uncertain Times

We've covered the fundamentals, which remain the same in boom and bust times, and in uncertain times. Uncertain times can provide the best opportunities. However, more planning care must be taken. Every well-planned investment and acquisition real estate transaction goes through a series of steps:

1) Goals setting;
2) Planning;
3) Locating properties;
4) Making offers;
5) Negotiating the contract;
6) Removing contingencies;
7) Closing.

Let's look at each step in detail.

1. GOAL SETTING

People can be effective without setting goals, but I find that part of life's pleasure is setting one's sights on specific targets and then taking steps to achieve them. There are many metaphors on the subject, including comparing the journey embarked upon without goals to the ship setting sail without a rudder.

In real estate investing and estate building, goal setting is necessary to determine why the investor wants to invest in real estate and that usually has to do with making money. A typical real estate investment goal might be to make a million dollars in ten years, using real estate investments. Whatever the goal, the investor needs to create a plan to accomplish it and break the long term goal into a series of short-term goals.

Before commencing the planning step, it is necessary to make an in-depth, honest evaluation of the goals to be sure they are what we really want. The determining factor of whether we will accomplish our goals is how much of a COMMITMENT we are willing to make to fulfill them. In attempting to accomplish anything worthwhile, we will run into problems and obstacles, and the player without real commitment will quit, while the truly motivated person will solve the problems and overcome the obstacles.

The next question to consider is whether the goals have been set too high or too low? Maybe we really want more, but our belief system will not allow us to dream lofty dreams. A good exercise in goal setting is to make a list of 100 things we don't have in our lives that we would, deep-down, like to have. Then place a price tag and time limit on achieving each one. These costs, combined with the everyday expenses of living, and the extraordinary costs of such things as children's college education, will determine what the player's monetary goals are. When I went through this exercise, I had to raise my long term goals by over 60%. But, in doing it, I knew what I wanted and, more importantly, WHY I wanted it.

2. PLANNING

Next comes planning. The original plan to make a million in ten years may go something like this: I will invest $20,000 in a duplex, renovate it, get the rents up and increase the value by $30,000. I will make a tax deferred exchange for a six-unit, renovate it, raise the rents, increase my equity to $100,000 and exchange into a 15-unit. I will accomplish this in the first three years. After I have used my talents to increase the 15-unit value by $100,000, I will move my now $200,000 equity into a parcel of shopping center land, develop a small shopping center and increase my equity to $500,000. That $500,000 equity will go into a self-storage warehouse development project, which, when completed and filled with tenants, will give me equity of $1,000,000.

That may be a very workable plan. But, the motivated subconscious may come up with an even better and easier plan. So, we need to make an original plan, and then keep our eyes open for opportunities and our mind receptive to other and additional ideas.

And, we also need to be aware that the journey to the goal is the job of life. The goals, when achieved, may prove empty, or at best will only give us temporary satisfaction. But, having fun with the process of achieving, of solving the problems, of overcoming the obstacles, is what makes estate-building, with real estate as the vehicle, such a rewarding experience. Konstantinos Kavafis set out to explore this theme in his poem, Ithaca. It's possible, he wrote, that the most Ithaca has to offer is the journey to reach her. So, go to Ithaca, but do not ignore her gifts—the experiences, challenges and adventures found along the way.

3. LOCATING PROPERTIES

For the investor, a hard-charging, knowledgeable, honest real estate broker is an invaluable asset. As previously discussed, if the investor can find such a person, the investor should be absolutely loyal to the broker. This means that when another agent tells the investor about a property, the investor immediately informs the agent that he/she is already being represented by a broker and that the agent should contact his/her broker to present any properties. Should the investor spot a property in the paper or a sign on a building, instead of contacting the advertiser or owner directly, the loyal investor tells his/her broker to contact the advertiser or owner.

One of the best ways to alienate a broker is to chisel on commissions. The intelligent investor will hope to make his/her broker rich, knowing that in doing so, the investor too will become much richer.

Should the investor not be able to engage such a broker and be forced to locate properties on one's own, then several choices are open. The internet is the most obvious option. This is also one of the quickest ways to understand market prices. Start by calling on ads, then inspecting properties and comparing cap rates. It's a good policy to keep a record of all properties inspected. The record should include: price per square foot, cap rate, age, neighborhood, financing, and, for apartment buildings, the gross multiplier (the list price divided by the gross income), the date inspected and who showed it.

If the plan calls for the player to acquire a duplex, the player should learn the neighborhoods where duplexes are located and drive those neighborhoods looking for opportunities. This doesn't mean just looking for signs that the property is for sale, but also look for indications that the property is distressed. Weeds growing wild, unpainted trim and junk in the yard all indicate there might be a problem—and a motivated owner.

If the plan calls for locating a motel to convert to offices, a drive down all of the old highways and through the downtown areas where older motels are located should be a weekly run.

When a likely property is located, the player can find the ownership through the tax assessor's office or through a title company. In California and certain other states, title companies have customer service departments which can assist in locating ownership.

In chaotic times, a major source of available-to-purchase properties is lenders, who actively attempt to market properties taken back through foreclosure, possibly at bargain prices. These lenders sometimes will make "sweetheart deals," which could include low down payments and below market interest rates, to get their lender-foreclosed properties off their books. Most banks and savings and loan associations now call these properties REOs (real estate owned) or OREOs (other real estate owned). Each of the larger lenders has a department that handles the disposition of their REOs. The player should get to know all of these lenders in his/her community and keep current on what they have available.

Some lenders are much easier to work with than others. Some will not move from "market" price, while others will discount heavily. Some have very few REOs and are financially quite healthy. These lenders are less likely to make as many concessions as those with huge REO portfolios who might be in danger of having the Federal Home Loan Bank or Federal Reserve close them down. Lenders in this unfortunate position have been known to make some unbelievable deals.

Another property source is the business or legal newspaper foreclosure notices. If a property owner is about to lose his/her equity, it is often possible to pick the property up well below market. A good plan in these circumstances is to offer something other than cash for the owner's equity (vehicle, note, etc.) and use the available cash to cure the loans and to do whatever renovation work is necessary.

There are many "favorite" ways to locate properties, and each investor will develop his/her own specialty. The important thing is to get started—and act.

4. MAKING OFFERS

As often stated in this book, a good broker is an invaluable asset. The broker can greatly assist in determining what to offer, and how to offer it. And, I have found, it is much more comfortable making a low offer through an intermediary than to present it personally.

Remember, the big money in real estate investing is made buying low and selling high. Before making an offer, the player must feel comfortable that the property being considered has both ingredients. Just being able to purchase the property at the right price is not enough. The potential for growth must be present.

Once the criteria are met, the details of the offer must be worked out. The price is important, but the terms may be even more so. In a highly leveraged situation, the interest rate and how and when the interest is to be paid can make the difference between the player being able to make a successful investment or losing the property through foreclosure. Buyers have very little control over what an institutional lender will charge and how the loan is to be repaid, but the buyer can have a great deal to say about whether the seller will carry back notes on reasonable terms.

The only good time to negotiate outstanding seller financing terms is during the purchase negotiations. This is when the buyer can elect not to purchase the property if the terms are not to his/her satisfaction. The seller then must look at whether he/she really wants to sell. The best buys are made from motivated sellers. Motivated sellers will make concessions to move their properties.

The investor should be prepared to make offers on several different properties before he/she obtains an acceptance or an acceptable counteroffer. Do not fall in love with a property to the extent that price and terms become unimportant. Only occasionally does a property appear on the market that warrants a full price, all cash offer. I have seen properties with multiple all-cash offers for tens of thousands OVER the list price. In these cases, either the property was vastly under-priced, or a feeding frenzy was caused by a severe shortage of that type of property. I truly dislike attempting to acquire properties of that type in a seller's market.

It is important that the investor not be so greedy that he/she will never get an offer accepted. In the late 1970's, mid 1980s and late 1990s, and years 2000-2006 when California houses were appreciating 1% per month, many investors left fortunes on the table by continually trying to buy at yesterday's prices. On the other hand, many investors lost everything jumping on the speculation bandwagon when selling prices outdistanced what users could afford to pay.

There is no magic formula to determine what price to offer. I once had a client who read somewhere that you should always offer 10% less than the asking price. I have seen many properties where 30% under the asking price was too high and others where the asking price was a steal.

Most sellers expect some negotiation. They might even feel that they made a mistake on their listed price if they are offered full price. The bottom line is to offer price and terms that, after the negotiations are completed, leave both seller and buyer pleased.

The buyer should leave room for negotiation. A buyer will often place a "front porch" in an offer, a request that they expect to lose through negotiation. Sometimes the front porch is not rejected by the seller, and the buyer has made an even better deal than anticipated. An example of a "front porch" might be a buyer requesting the seller to forgive interest on a carry-back loan for a year.

The investor needs to set time limits in which to acquire his/her first property, and then subsequent properties. He/she needs to structure the purchase offer at a price below that which he/she feels makes the property a very good buy (based on comparables).

The property must have potential for growth. The terms must be such that the buyer can live with the payments and handle a reasonable amount of rent loss.

The offer must contain contingencies that will permit the property to be thoroughly checked out (due-diligence). If institutional financing is to be obtained or assumed, it is imperative that the offer be subject to buyer obtaining financing at an acceptable rate.

The offer must provide for a long enough period of escrow to permit all of the contingencies to be removed and all of the loan processing completed. However, it should not be so long that the seller feels that he/she doesn't have a real transaction. A 60 to 90 day escrow is customary, except on development deals or conversions when a considerably longer period may be necessary.

5. NEGOTIATING

The offer when presented is most often not acceptable. Sometimes the objections are minor, in which case the negotiations are minimal. Very often there are areas that are totally not acceptable to the seller, called "deal points." Should the parties not be able to negotiate these deal points, the transaction will fail.

This is the moment when a good broker can really earn his/her fee. The creative broker has been through many transactions, has structured around many objections, and very often has a solution that will satisfy both parties. I am convinced that, given a willing buyer and a willing seller, both motivated, I, as a broker, can structure and close any transaction.

Most real estate transactions start out relatively simple. They become complicated in working out solutions during negotiations. Three and four-way exchanges are born this way. No sane broker or principal starts out to make a four-way exchange. They evolve because a simple sale wouldn't work, then a two and three-way exchange failed, and it took a four-way exchange to get each principal the benefits he/she wanted.

Principals negotiating for their own account must remain flexible, open-minded and keep a sense of humor if they expect to be successful. Clients have accused me of being too concerned about the other principal's position. But, I know that a successful transaction depends upon an understanding of the benefits the other party needs in order to close. Every real estate transaction must be a win-win situation or it will not close; or, if it does, it will end in litigation. Each party's position must be respected, and the negotiation should take place in a context of everyone getting the benefits they seek.

I don't believe any offer should be flatly rejected. If one party takes the time to make an offer, no matter how insulting, the other party should have the courtesy to counter that offer. Then, the first party should counter that counter. Only if the parties are so far apart that no one can possibly figure how to make the deal work should a transaction be dropped.

THE CONTRACT

In different parts of the country, the final real estate purchase or exchange contract takes different forms. And, the size and complexity of the transaction will also determine the contract form. The purchase of a house or small apartment building in Northern California will normally be handled with a "Deposit Receipt" and a set of escrow instructions drawn by the title company when the transaction is ready to close. In Southern California and Arizona, escrow instructions are drawn early by an escrow company, usually when the parties reach a deal point agreement agreeing on all of the deal points.

Large, complicated transactions require real estate attorneys to create a detailed document.

It is very important to use a qualified real estate attorney. On two occasions, I have worked with attorneys whose work created major problems. One failed to properly document a deal point and the other failed to catch a very adverse clause placed in a lengthy contract by the other party's attorney. In both cases, the errors returned to haunt my principals.

The principal and broker cannot assume that the attorney has done the work properly. Every document needs to be reviewed to make sure the principal is getting what he/she bargained for.

LETTER OF INTENT

Many large transactions start with a letter of intent. A letter of intent outlines the terms and conditions under which a buyer will acquire a property, but it is not a binding document. If there is a general meeting of the minds, it will set forth a time when a formal contract will be prepared. The idea is to save the expense of having attorneys prepare documents for transactions with no chance of closing.

6. REMOVING CONTINGENCIES

With any transaction, both parties will usually have certain concerns and the contract is structured with contingencies that remove buyer's and seller's objections to signing. I prefer to get a contract signed by all parties to a transaction as early in the negotiations as possible. The underlying psychology is that once we obtain signatures, both parties, rather than continuing as adversaries, will become cooperative in trying to remove contingencies and move toward closing.

If the property is out of town and a buyer is nervous about signing an offer to purchase a property unseen, a contract can include the contingency: "subject to inspection and approval of the real estate." For income properties, offers may be subject to inspection and approval of the rent rolls, income and expense statements for the previous two years. Other contingencies include acquiring party's approval of loans, preliminary title reports (or abstract of title), leases, a contractor's structural inspection, a Phase 1, toxic clearance and a termite clearance.

Once the parties agree and sign, the only thing standing in the way of closing is getting the contingencies removed and the title company to insure. Almost all real estate transactions should have title insurance. I have never been involved in a transaction where the insurance company has had to pay off, but the due diligence they perform in order to be able to insure good title to the property uncovers most problems.

Each contingency needs to have someone working on getting it handled. If a broker is involved, the broker will direct the closing, assigning responsibilities. A broker-less transaction will require the principals to handle it themselves. A checklist should be made up with the responsible party's name beside the function and an agreed upon date for completion of each step.

7. CLOSING

Fun time! It all comes together: money, deeds, and all of the documents to be signed are brought together at the title company, the escrow company, or the attorney's office. Assuming all contingencies have been removed and the title company is comfortable that everything is in order and is prepared to insure title, then the transaction is ready to record and, upon recording, title and money pass hands.

Closing is both the end and the beginning: the end of search and negotiation, and the beginning of management and creation of value.

Chapter 14
Winning Investment Strategy

Boom times, bust times and uncertain times beyond, we have come full circle. We started with the developer pronouncing, "It's all in the timing." We covered cap rates and cash on cash returns and leverage. Readers have a basic understanding of financing, property management and exchanging, pyramiding and estate building. We know the qualities to look for when choosing team members and the steps required to close transactions. This final chapter will be devoted to covering the important lessons I have learned in my 40 plus years buying, selling, brokering, developing and building real properties.

I have made and lost two fortunes in real estate and, at this writing, I am building my third. I have tried the stock market, and for a short period of time worked for a Fortune 500 company. Aside from those short transgressions, my entire working life has been in real estate.

During those periods without income and with no closings on the horizon, I have questioned my career choice. But then, when I get involved in an exciting, creative transaction and find myself fully consumed by my work, I realize that I wouldn't trade careers with anyone.

Real estate deals are fun. The people who make their living brokering, developing, building or actively investing for a living are a fascinating bunch. Most of us are dropouts from other professions; some couldn't cut it elsewhere, but many more who simply enjoy living by our wits.

And then there is the elusive, but ever-sought, giant pot of gold at the end of the rainbow. Never mind that many of the most adventuresome real estate entrepreneurs die broke. The ride was worth the price.

The life we live is exciting. It isn't drudgery getting up and going to work. Quite the contrary, many of us have to be dragged away from our offices and computers. I have liked playing golf and tennis, flying my plane and skiing, but there is nothing more exciting than putting together a difficult, creative real estate transaction.

The problem is that many of us so like the creative part of playing the game that we sometimes ignore the fundamentals. And that will ultimately cause us to go broke.

To review, here are some of the more important fundamentals with a sprinkling of do's and don'ts thrown in.

PLAYING THE CYCLES
Position yourselves to take advantage of the economy. Avoid getting caught up in the buying frenzy of a sellers' market. Even though it may seem like boom times will never end, they will. No area of the country is immune to a boom or a bust.

Real estate can be bought for speculation and fortunes have been made doing so, but nearly as many have been lost by those who didn't get out before it was too late. One way to avoid being caught in a speculative craze is to keep rational contact with the real world of real estate. Are homes being speculated to a point where those that intend to occupy can no longer afford to buy or to qualify for a loan? If so, then it's time to get off that bandwagon.

Are shopping centers and office building cap rates becoming so low (prices so high in relation to income) that investors are better off in the bond market? In order for a property to make economic sense, do rents need to be raised beyond an amount that tenants can afford?

All of these conditions occurred just before the bottom fell out of the California real estate market in 1989 and again in 2006.

Conversely, in times of recession, don't let the doom and gloom people convince you that real estate will never again become a good investment. It will. There is only a fixed amount of real property, but more and more people inhabit this country, and this planet. Obviously, worldwide population growth shouldn't be the sole criterion for making a buying decision. But when rates of return make sense, real estate is again ready to take its place as the most opportune of all investments. If interest rates are at 8% and the bond market yields 7%, then a small strip center that will yield 10% offers the clear investment advantage, just from a yield standpoint. Factor in leverage, the potential for appreciation and the tax benefits and real estate will outperform the stock and bond market every time.

So lesson one is play the cycles.

LOCATION

Location, location, location. This has always been a fundamental and when ignored, can prove disastrous. The search for the right location starts with the right city, and progresses to the right neighborhood, and finally the right street or right corner. Shopping center developers will tell you that the "going-home corner" will do a better business than the "going-to-work corner."

The prudent investor will make sure that the city has positive prospects. Rising employment and new industry make for a bright future, but often a better buy can be made before everyone else jumps on the bandwagon. Certain cities will always come back. Because of location,

San Francisco and New York will never dry up and blow away. Because of climate, San Diego, Los Angeles, Phoenix, Miami and Honolulu will always rebound from recessions and will draw people and employers. Las Vegas will not die, at least not in our lifetimes. Gambling will see to that.

But certain neighborhoods in those cities have become war zones and although fortunes can be made in those areas, the investor must be realistic about his or her abilities to deal with gangs, drug dealers and crime before considering ownership there.

When evaluating location, the investor must take an objective look at the location-price trade off. Better locations are priced higher than those with lesser appeal. Many top locations demand such a price premium that the return on the investment makes no economic sense. Buyers of properties in those locations often purchase for reasons that are not economic, at least not in the short-term. Often these buyers like the status of owning a "trophy" building.

In addition to the prestige purchasers, certain long-view investors will purchase an irreplaceable property for a seemingly absurd price, believing that it will appreciate over time, like a fine work of art.

Japanese investors tend to take the long-view, and while in many cases their approach has proven successful, they have often so overpaid that if just the average compounding of money were computed, they can't possibly make a profit.

Most of us don't have the luxury of buying solely for the long-term, so we attempt to make the best deal we can based on today's income and a property's profit potential over the next one to five years. With that criteria, take a very objective look at the location-price trade-off. Are we buying that location just because it is cheap, or will the location really stand the test of time?

RISK / REWARD EVALUATION

Before shooting craps with one's life savings, risk must be measured. And it must be measured against potential reward. Over the years, I have blissfully signed millions of dollars of notes and, in nearly all cases, have paid the money back on time.

Not all of my ventures have been successful. I relearned the correlation between risk and reward during the recession of the early 1990s, which found me with six unsold custom homes and a business venture that drained me of two years of productivity and the last of my savings. The notes and contracts that I signed when everything looked rosy became a very heavy burden.

My price for this lesson, though painful, was minor compared to some of my friends. Many not only lost everything they had accumulated over 30 to 40 years, but spent endless days and weeks in court and some even spent time in jail.

Since childhood, we all have taken risks for a variety of reasons. We have taken stupid dares and tackled heroic challenges. In business, risk should be measured for its probable and possible economic results. This is not necessarily the only criteria for measuring risk, but without question, the potential economic upside and downside should be measured and understood before proceeding with any business venture.

My worst business decisions resulted from not fully evaluating the downside potential for disaster. I financially buried a former good friend and client in a deal that neither one of us should ever have been involved in. With a third party, we formed a partnership and my friend/client pledged a million dollar note for the partnership to acquire a resort property. But that was only the beginning. Next, all three of us personally guaranteed some bank loans. The investment failed to live up to expectations and began costing the partnership $30,000 per month. We poured in hundreds of thousands of dollars in cash and, when that well ran dry, we became obligated for hundreds of thousands more from a line of credit.

Had I really thought through what might happen, we never would have done the deal in the first place. In retrospect, I didn't even make the deal for economic reasons. Oh yes, I expected we would make a profit, but the projected profit was never sufficient for the risk inherent with all of the required guarantees. No, the reason I made the deal was because I wanted to be in business with the other two partners and the resort was a vehicle to do so.

Personal guarantees and cross-collateralizating loans can destroy your net worth. A deal would have to be nearly foolproof (is that possible?) before I would ever consider either again.

PARTNERSHIPS

As a developer and builder, I have been in numerous building and development partnerships. As a syndicator, I have formed several invest-ment partnerships. And I have partnered to acquire and operate prop-erties and businesses. About 75% of my partnerships have made money; the other 25% have not. When everything is going well, partnerships are very pleasant relationships. When things go bad—well, then you begin to see the best and worst in people.

Here are some thoughts regarding partnerships:
- Partnerships and partners must be very carefully considered. With the possible exception of marriages, more friendships are lost through partnerships than any other way.
- Don't become partners with anyone you don't like and espe-cially with someone you don't trust.
- Every partnership aspect should be in writing. The expectations of each party, not only with regards to money, but time commitment and duties to be performed must be clearly understood, agreed upon, and documented. Because no deal ever goes as planned, it is imperative that each party be clear as to their responsibilities.

- Never partner with anyone who is not willing to be responsible for his/her own actions. A "victim" partner will blame you for everything going wrong.
- Never partner with anyone who is investing or obligating more than he/she can comfortably afford to lose. Each partner must understand and accept the risk.
- Only partner with people who have a sense of humor and do not take themselves or their circumstances too seriously.

HOMEWORK

Discussing our most glaring business errors while on a run in the Mexican jungle, my friend Dan Murr, a very successful syndicator, related that his misstep had been the result of incomplete homework. As we made our way along the twisting trail, he explained that although he had always performed meticulous due diligence when acquiring properties for his partnerships, he had not been as thorough on the trailer park he had purchased for his own account. He had failed to properly ensure that he was excused from personal liability (in a personal liability state), and that error had cost him dearly.

Thorough homework requires obtaining all of the information and understanding it. In purchasing an income property, the minimum that any investor must be comfortable with is:
- The guarantee of good title to the property;
- A complete and accurate accounting of all income and expenses, including any tenant concessions;
- Copies of all leases and documents affecting the property;
- An understanding of current tenant intentions, whether they are happy and intend to stay and whether any landlord promises have been made.
- Any environmental, structural or infestation problems;
- All loan documents and lenders rights; and
- Zoning conformity, and city, county or state agency violations.

If the information is not available, or if it is not understood, it could be very foolish to proceed. Problems with toxins and asbestos can render some properties unsalable. Vacating tenants can cause severe financial problems. Violations of city ordinances or non-permitted uses can result in building and business closures. Lenders have called in loans and foreclosed when loans are not properly assumed.

In most cases, none of the above will be a problem. Often, deficiencies can be solved in escrow, during the due diligence period. But, when any of the above escapes notice, the investor can be severely damaged.

Do your homework—get the information and thoroughly understand it.

COOKIE CUTTERS VS ADVENTURERS

I met Barnie and Ron while waiting on a TV soundstage, preparing to do a pilot for a talk show. Our discussion came around to our real estate successes and failures and here is what we discovered.

Barnie and I were adventurers. We had plenty of ups and downs in our real estate careers. We were easily bored and when we got good at something, we found a new thing to try. Consequently, we failed a lot.

Ron, on the other hand, had enjoyed steady success. He made a very successful career out of buying run-down houses, rehabbing them and then renting them or reselling them at a profit. He knew his market, could spot a good buy, knew the costs involved to rehab and the rental income a place could bring. He had established a rapport with lenders and was very active in his community. He did the same deal over and over—a cookie cutter.

I believe that Ron's way is the surest way to continually make money in real estate. Find a formula that works for you, perfect it, polish it and then repeat it.

CHANGES: Boom, Bust and Beyond

Real estate is constantly changing. It once took one day to get a building permit and only six weeks for subdivision approval: many of my fellow 'old timer' developers are unwilling to go through the two year plus hassle now required for the same approvals.

Change has also discouraged brokers and investors. The one page purchase agreement has grown into ten pages of legal small print. Attorneys lurk, waiting for opportunities to sue. Homes that once sold for $10,000 now require more than that for a down payment, and apartment houses command twice the purchase price as ten years ago. Federal regulators change financing rules; the EPA sets toxic and asbestos traps.

Yes, things change, but those changes provide opportunities for new players who are willing to learn and play by the new rules.

Real estate opportunities are not going to disappear. Individuals, families, businesses, and governments all require real estate. With the world's population growth, expanding economies and exploding technology, new and profitable opportunities will continue to present themselves to alert and creative players.

The real estate game is a wonderful hands-on game, where the player determines his or her own fate—adult Monopoly, played for real money. Unlike the stock market, the real estate investor is not at the mercy of someone else's management. The player gets to make the decisions.

The real estate game offers delightful interactions with team members: buyers, sellers, attorneys, accountants, title people and lenders. The product is something that can be seen and touched.

Played humanely, the real estate game can enhance people's lives. Tenants and homebuyers can experience an improved lifestyle, office and factory workers better working conditions, and all of us a more beautiful and inviting environment.

Tap your creativity and explore your limits. From designing transactions to designing buildings and doing land planning, there is space to let your talents explode.

There is room in the real estate game for all types of players, from the adventurer to the cookie-cutter, the conservative to the crap shooter. The active player can buy, sell, wheel and deal, manage and develop, while the aloof player can take a more passive role.

I love real estate. From the excitement of buying, selling, brokering and developing to the challenge of solving difficult real estate problems and putting together complicated exchanges, this game is heady stuff. And there is always something new to learn, and always a bigger game to play.

During boom times, bust times and the unknown times beyond, real estate is the best game in town.

About the Author

Chester W. "Chet" Allen, CCIM, is a graduate of Stanford University with a degree in Economics.

A licensed real estate broker since 1965, Mr. Allen has successfully brokered over $110 million in closings, including some of the most complex transactions in history. One exchange transaction, involving 35 principals and 12 lenders, concurrently closed escrow on 64 properties, located in three time zones, stretching from coast to coast.

He is the only broker to receive both of the nation's two most prestigious commercial real estate awards; the Campbell Trophy for the Best Commercial-Investment Transaction in the United States, and the Snyder Trophy for the Best Exchange in the United States. The California Association of Realtors has honored him four times for brokering California's Most Outstanding Investment Transactions.

The author holds the designation, Certified Commercial Investment Member (CCIM), commercial real estate's highest, is past president of the National Society of Exchange Counselors, and has been inducted in the Exchangor's Hall of Fame.

As a developer, building designer and licensed general contractor, Mr. Allen has designed, built and marketed housing subdivisions, apartment complexes, condominiums, office and industrial buildings.

He has written extensively for Creative Real Estate, a magazine for real estate professionals, and has received their Best Creator of Wealth Award.

Mr. Allen has created and conducted heavily attended seminars throughout the United States (approved for Realtor's continuing education by state agencies) on the topics of Analyzing Investment Properties, Developing and Syndication, Client Estate Building, The Secrets of Successful Exchanging, and Beyond 1031, Market Driven Exchanging. On three occasions he has been guest lecturer at Stanford University's Graduate School of Engineering.